PIZZ&
LO♥E

DESIGN & PHOTOGRAPHY BY DAVE BROWN

Hardie Grant

QUADRILLE

James and Thom at
the legendary Joe's
in NYC.

Introduction

Grab a slice.

Since our original Pizza Pilgrimage through Italy in 2011, we have now been obsessing about pizza for 11 years. In that time we have hand stretched countless pizza bases, sliced literally tonnes of mozzarella and blitzed litres of Italian tomatoes.

More than this, we have also employed a small army of pizza chefs to work in our growing collection of Pizza Pilgrims pizzerias across the UK. Our chefs are amazing for two main reasons. Firstly, they all bring amazing energy and passion to their work, something that is evident in the quality of pizzas they make day in day out in the pizzerias. Secondly, they all bring a little tip, a little insight and a little flourish that improves pizza making for the whole company. Over the years, the list of these tips and tricks has grown longer and longer. Pizza making is genuinely a skill that can take a lifetime to master.

What is also evident, as a result of the dreaded lockdown, is that so many people started on their own pizza-making journey while stuck at home. Sales of home pizza ovens went through the roof, and people had all the fermenting time they needed to discover the art of great pizza dough.

After the success of our book *Pizza* in 2020, we wanted to provide these new pizza recruits with all the knowledge they need to perfect the craft in one handy little package. As such, we are delighted to present *Slice*!

Slice is a distillation of our original book with a focus on recipes, pizza making advice and detailed explorations of key pizza ingredients. It is perfect for someone with a new found love of pizza making, to help them get the best out of their new pizza oven and make sure it doesn't just gather dust in the shed! It is also a source of more detail for those looking for it – unpacking things like dough fermentation strategy and contentious ingredients to experiment with! All tied up in a small, splash-proof book for easy use in the kitchen and the garden.

From Neapolitan classics like Salsiccia e Friarielli, to more multicultural creations like Double Pepperoni and Spicy Honey, we really hope you enjoy making these pizzas as much as we have. This book is a slice of everything we have learned about pizza over the last 11 years. Bring on the next 11!

Please do share any pizza making tips, tricks and recipes of your own with us at pizzabook@pizzapilgrims.co.uk. Who knows, maybe your recipe could be one of our next pizzeria guest specials.

Pizza and love,

Thom and James

Zuppardi's, home of the best clam pie in New Haven. These two have been coming here every Thursday for 23 years.

Tomatoes

We use different varieties of tomatoes in the pizzerias: one for sauce and the other for keeping whole and using as a topping.

SAN MARZANO

The story goes that the tomato seed was given by the Viceroyalty of Peru to the King of Naples in 1770 as a gift. It was planted in the small town of San Marzano sul Sarno, just outside Naples.

This town is nestled in the foothills of Vesuvius, where the soils are incredibly fertile. San Marzano tomatoes are considered by many to be the best sauce tomatoes in the world and, as such, are protected under Italian law or DOP. These tomatoes have thick flesh, few seeds and thin skins. The thin skins allow them to make the most of the Naples climate, soaking up the sun and in turn having a sweet and aromatic flavour.

The recipe we are asked most for in the pizzerias is our tomato sauce recipe. The truth is, it's the easiest recipe we have. We take great-quality canned tomatoes and mill them by hand through a wide sieve. We mill them this way for two reasons: firstly, it gives the sauce a great texture with actual pieces of tomato flesh (not completely broken down, like a passata); secondly, the seeds of a tomato are bitter, so if you blend them in a food processor that bitterness will go into the sauce – by hand milling we prevent the seeds from being blitzed and adding bitterness. The only ingredient we add to the tomatoes is salt. After that, it just gets a 60-second flash in the oven on the pizza. And there you have it – a sweet, salty, aromatic sauce that is fresh and full of flavour.

DATTERİNİ

We only use one other kind of tomato in the pizzerias: beautiful datterini tomatoes from Sicily. The word 'datterini' literally means 'little dates', and they're named as such on account of their intense sweetness, small size and elongated shape. They have thick skins, making them really robust, and few seeds, meaning more flesh! We use them as a topping on some of our pizzas. The other very noticeable characteristic of datterini tomatoes is their incredible aroma – add the stalks to sauces to impart a super floral flavour.

Fior di latte & Mozzarella

James was working for free at Di Matteo pizzeria in Naples just before we started Pizza Pilgrims. The mozzarella supplier arrived on his Vespa with the day's mozzarella. He put down his espresso, signalled for James to come over and said,

'You the English guy?'

'Yup...'

'Taste this mozzarella!'

It was unlike any mozzarella we'd tried before. You could taste the fresh milk and acidity, and the texture was tougher than we are used to in the UK, with more elasticity and bite.

'You will never get mozz like this in London.'

And he was right. The mozzarella you get in Naples, and which is made and eaten on the same day, is something worth travelling for. We work really hard to get our mozzarella to our pizzerias as quickly as is humanly possible but, the truth is, it still takes days. There's something quite comforting to know that however hard we try to make the best pizza, it will never be quite as good as in Naples. We're OK with that; they did invent it.

It is worth noting, that when it comes to discussing Mozzarella in the context of Neapolitan Pizza, you could be talking about two different products. The first is 'fior di latte', which is the mozzarella used as standard on a Neapolitan Margherita and which is made with cow's milk (the name translated means 'flower of milk'). Mozzarella made with buffalo milk is referred to as 'bufala' (or 'Mozzarella di Bufala Campana' to give it the full name). This distinction is a really important one as bufala is a much creamier, wetter product than fior di latte. Make sure you ask specifically for bufala in Naples if that is what you would like on your pizza.

MAKİNG YOUR OWN FİOR Dİ LATTE MOZZARELLA

On the face of it, this could be seen as a really simple way to make cheese. And in many ways, it is. We've tried this a few times at home and you can create something that could only be described as mozzarella. However, as with so many Italian crafts, it takes a lifetime to master. So, who better to hand you over to for this process than our good friend, and owner of Latteria Sorrentina in Naples, Giovanni. This is how they make mozzarella the right way...

'The key to great mozzarella is twofold: the milk and the experience...'

1. We heat full-fat Italian milk (from grass-fed cows) gently with the microbiological rennet (ethical and suitable for vegetarians) until it's approximately 30–32°C/86–89°F. This lets the caseins separate from the wheys. The exact point of maturation for the curds is an art that comes with practice, and will in turn deliver the best cheese.

2. Once the curds have set, the heat is turned off and the cheese is cut.

3. The curds are left to cool in the whey and then are drained.

4. At this point, we begin the traditional process of 'spinning'. The curds are stirred together with some of the whey and heated to above 82°C/179°F. Traditionally, spinning is done in a wooden bowl with a long wooden spoon. The curds are placed in the bowl and then the whey is poured over the top. Using the spoon, you pull the curds into long stretches. Usually after 3–4 pulls the cheese will take on a shine and smoothness. The curds are then balled.

5. The balls are rested for at least 15 minutes in room-temperature salted water. This imparts a good saltiness to the mozzarella. It is important not to rest it in ice-cold water as you will end up with a tough and rubbery mozzarella.

6. Once rested, store in salted water until needed.

Note: Supermarket milk is pasteurised at temperatures of up to 138°C/276°F, which means that it cannot be made into mozzarella.

Left: Thom & James with The Mozzarella Kings, Giovanni Amodio and Franco Amodio.

Parmesan

One of Italy's hero products – which has secretly been living on your pizza all this time!

Parmesan is 100% identified with Italy and remains one the products that they are most proud of (and most reluctant to let leave their shores; the Italians are the masters of keeping the good stuff for themselves). Parmesan is so revered in Italy that you can use wheels of it as collateral against a bank loan!

Parmigiano-Reggiano (the name is derived from the two towns near to the home of its production, Parma and Reggio Emilia) is, on the face of it, a very simple product. It only contains three ingredients: milk, salt and rennet. But through the mysterious combination of expertise and, more importantly, time, it morphs into a product with incredible complexity, balance and flavour that you just wouldn't believe. It really is one of those products that, when you see it being made, makes you wonder how anyone discovered how great it would turn out in the end.

Milk is delivered to the factory twice a day, where the master cheese maker oversees its blending and cooking in preparation for the production of every individual Parmesan wheel. He is only paid for the ones that end up passing stringent tests after months of curing, so it's in his best interests to stay focused.

In order to be considered actual Parmesan, the cheese needs to cure for at least 12 months; however, the best Parmesan (with the fullest flavour and little protein deposits that make for a satisfying crunchiness) is cured for at least 36 months.

Every Parmesan supplier will always have a secret stash of cheese that has been aged even longer than this – that no one will ever get their hands on!

We visited a Parmesan production facility on our original pilgrimage and, let's just say, they took it pretty seriously. The maturing rooms contained about 25,000 wheels of Parmesan at various stages of maturation, at a total value of around ten million euros! So, we guess it's fair enough that they take it seriously.

We know what you are thinking; why is this relevant to pizza? Get to the point! Well, certainly in the case of traditional Neapolitan rules, Parmesan is added to almost every single pizza. It adds a great umami hit and complements the flavours on Neapolitan Margherita perfectly.

Divisive Ingredients

Ever since there have been people, there have been arguments as to what should, and what should not, go on their pizza. The arguments that are sparked over a pizza menu have ended friendships and marriages. We think it's fair to say these are some of the moments when people understand each other the least. Below is a list of some of the most divisive ingredients we've come across.

PİNEAPPLE

Pineapple on pizza was first created by a six-foot, long-haired Hawaiian surfer called Uluwehi... NAAAAAT! Despite its truly tropical name, the Hawaiian pizza was invented in the sixties by a retired Greek cook called Sam Panopoulos at the Satellite Restaurant in Chatham, Ontario. He said he just had some pineapple in stock so tried it on the pizza and, right from the get go, it divided opinion. He said: 'Some people loved it and others said "are you crazy?!"'. It's taken us a long time to come to terms with it, but, we can now proudly say that we love pineapple on pizza – and we will fight you over it! Even the god of pizza, Franco Pepe, has a pizza with pineapple on it!

PASTA

In Naples they really love two things: pizza and pasta. However, they very much take the 'too much of a good thing' mentality seriously and so the idea of pasta on pizza is sacrilegious. We learned this the hard way when we created a guest pizza for our menu featuring our other favourite dish, pasta carbonara. We topped a white pizza with olive oil, roasted pancetta, mozzarella, Parmesan, strands of bucatini pasta and egg yolk. There's no other way to describe it than jaw-droppingly DELICIOUS! On the day we launched it we got a number of calls and emails from our Neapolitan chefs asking for a 'serious chat' and in one case a threat of resignation. It took over a week to convince everyone that this was just for fun, and not a permanent feature on the menu. Thankfully no chefs left, and it ended up being one of our best-selling pizzas. Go figure!

Andrea Di Maio –
Pizza Pilgrims pizzaiolo.

ANCHOVIES

Now, even the Italians break their own rule here. You often hear in Italy, 'fish and cheese should never be eaten together!', but they flagrantly disregard this rule with anchovies. To understand why, you have to go back to the beginning (of pizza…). Pizza came into existence as a peasant food, and one of the toppings most abundantly available to the poor of southern Italy were anchovies. The Mediterranean was full of them and they could be preserved very easily in a little salt or oil. So, anchovies were first put on pizza for survival reasons, for essential protein. Since then, anchovies have remained synonymous with pizza but one that seems to put you in the 'weird food eater' category. The Olsen twins sing of their hate of anchovies on pizza in their infamous 'pizza rap', but they clearly cannot be trusted. On the other hand, Fry from *Futurama* spends a whole episode championing the little fish on pizza!

CHICKEN

Now, this one is a thinker. Every Italian worth their *sale* will run a mile at the idea of chicken on pizza. We've had this argument with our pizza chefs and they will shout until they are blue in the face, but can't actually give a reason as to why they're against it. We've trawled the internet and can't find any strong evidence to cling to. Perhaps the texture of chicken is too close to the dough? Maybe they are both performing the same job, acting as vehicles for flavour? Outside of Italy chicken on pizza seems to be loved the world over, with BBQ chicken being voted in the top three ingredients by Domino's customers in the US. We think this is just one of the rules we'll have to put in the same category as 'no cappuccinos after midday' – those that seem to happen for no reason but that Italians live and die by.

CURRY BANANA

This one is just plain bizarre, coming from glorious Sweden, the country that brought you *surströmming*, a putrefied canned fish that is so smelly it is illegal to open indoors. We tried the stuff once and it was the only time in our lives that we were able to *see* a smell! So, maybe it's not so surprising that one of the most popular pizzas in Sweden is a Margherita topped with sliced banana, curry powder and peanuts. We took the time to make this with our chefs, hoping it would be like a twist on a Hawaiian… it was not. It tasted like a smoothie on a pizza but with added curry. We dare you, next time you're making pizza at home, grab a banana and some curry powder and… completely ruin it!

'THERE İS NO ASPECT, NO FACET, NO MOMENT OF LİFE THAT CAN'T BE İMPROVED WİTH PİZZA.'

DARIA

Making Pizza at Home

We are living in unprecedented times people! It wasn't too long ago that your best bet for making pizza at home was either dropping £5k on a full-blown, brick pizza oven or popping the box on a frozen pizza and waiting 16 minutes for a paradoxically crispy and doughy, tomato-ketchup mess that would burn the roof of your mouth. How glorious it is to live in a modern age where home pizza perfection is so easily available!

ROCCBOX

If Steve Jobs designed a pizza oven, this would be it. The Roccbox reminds us of the early iMacs for their sleek design. For us, this oven replicates the conditions of our Neapolitan pizza ovens the best. The gas fire gives a great char and the stone floor allows the crust to rise beautifully. An even bigger seal of approval is that we've noticed a lot of street food traders and restaurants using these in their kitchens – confirmation that it's a hard worker!

COB OVEN

So, just a heads up, you are going to need some space for this one! It's hard to say whether this is more art project than operation-pizza-oven but it's fun to do and you feel like a hero once it's done. This is how we did it: First thing you need is some clay-rich soil (we Googled where in London has clay soil and then drove around until we found some roadworks – after asking nicely, they let us shovel an Ikea bag's worth of soil into the car). Next, you need to get some sand and straw, which we easily got from the local hardware store. Lay out a tarpaulin in the garden and then mix together about two-parts clay soil, one-part sand and one-part straw. You then add as much water as you need to make a thick clay cement. Much like crushing grapes, you can use your feet to squelch the clay together until you have a nice smooth and consistent cement. Next, take some fire bricks (which you can order online) and arrange them in a circle on a flat (preferably concrete) outdoor surface. Then mix some more sand with a little water so it sticks together and start piling it up to create a tall and round mound in the centre of your bricks, leaving about 10cm/4in around the internal edge. Cover the sand with pages of wet newspaper to create a solid(ish) dome shape. Take your clay cement and begin to cover the sand mound entirely. You should aim for a 10cm/4in

James' first oven, made out of a bin, some mud and a tennis ball tube.

depth all the way around. Once totally covered, cut a mouth in your oven where you want the front to be, big enough to slide a pizza through. The mouth should be two-thirds of the height of the internal dome height to allow for good air flow. Allow to dry for a couple of hours then use your hand to dig out all of the sand and – ta-da! – you have a pizza oven. Leave it another few hours to dry a little more, then light a small fire in the oven. This will fire the clay and solidify the oven. Add wood to the fire slowly until you have a larger fire and then leave to burn out overnight. The next day you are ready to make pizza! Easy!

PIZZA STONE

Hmmm... the pizza stone. As heavy as it is *terrible* at making great pizza. At about £30 a pop we can see why so many people bought them. But, here's the problem: they get too hot for shop-bought pizzas and not hot enough for homemade pizzas. When you drop a homemade pizza with raw dough onto a pizza stone the temperature immediately drops and a 200°C/400°F/Gas 6 oven just doesn't have enough fire power to give the pizza the nice crisp bottom it deserves and to allow the crust to rise properly. Our advice is, if you want to cook pizza this way, then just go to your local building shop and buy a stone slab for two quid. Dodge the branded kit – it's a rip-off!

FRYING PAN PIZZA

OK, bias warning... this is our method! We came up with this technique in the first week we started Pizza Pilgrims. We'd just got our van with the pizza oven back from the oven manufacturer and invited 50 friends round as a test run. In our naivety, we lit the oven way too late and the pizzas were coming out looking anaemic. So, we got a pan screaming hot on the hob, dropped the pizza in the pan and instantly the crust rose and the bottom browned beautifully. We finished the pizza under a hot grill (broiler) and the party was saved. We know we're biased, but we think this method wins hands down. It creates a beautiful, light and fluffy pizza and all you need is a frying pan, which costs about £15. Pizza to the people! See our full method on page 39.

Check out that CRUST!

Pulling this expression is optional.

PİZZA DOUGH İS ALİVE

By Pizza Pilgrims' First Chef Tom Mullin

There is nothing more debated within pizza than dough. It's the first thing pizza fanatics like us will look at. It's what we constantly think about and what we reminisce about. If I think back to the best slice of pizza I've ever had, sure I remember the sweet tomato and the creamy mozzarella, but what I can really recall is the dough and its pillows of crust seasoned with those toppings. The crust, which has been charred with attitude, giving just a slight chewiness, melting in your mouth, leaves you eager for another slice. That's Neapolitan pizza.

Usually made with very few ingredients but with a fierce amount of accuracy and a complex simplicity. One of the coolest things I've learned while obsessing over pizza is that as chefs (*pizzaiolo* in Italian) we are literally creating and capturing life in the form of dough – introducing water to flour, with the help of living yeast cells, we mould and nurture. Our dough is a living and very much breathing thing.

Neapolitan pizza dough relies on only the basic bread ingredients of flour, water, salt and yeast, but like we've found in many southern Italian recipes, what makes the difference is how the ingredients are used. A simple recipe becomes so much more when you take a closer look at how precisely the ingredients are balanced by a pizzaiolo.

With that balance there is one more very significant ingredient which often gets overlooked, and that is time. Time is probably the greatest and most important ingredient in making dough. In some way, similar to us, dough needs time to mature and develop.

FLOUR

Flour is the most abundant ingredient in our dough and really sets the tone for the rest of the pizza, so we'll need to give it plenty of attention. Our goal is to make a soft and long-rising dough. There will be many variables in achieving this, but when it comes to flour the two main attributes are the grain fineness and the strength.

Grain Fineness

In pizza and pasta dough recipes we often see this term double zero or '00'. It has good reason to be so beloved in the pizza world, but first we need to understand what makes flour 'double zero'.

Italy has a numerical system for grading flours which is 2, 1, 0 and 00, and these indicate how fine the flour is milled. Grade 2 is the coarser end of the scale, which is comparable to wholewheat or brown flour. As we go down the numbers, the flour is milled more and more until 00, which is ground to an extreme fineness. So fine it's almost like a dust. It's this 00 flour which gives a silky-smooth feel to the classic Neapolitan pizza dough.

Strength

Protein equals strength, and to explain what that means we're going to get a little bit scientific. When mixed with water, protein molecules in the flour bind together to produce strands of gluten. The network of gluten strands form strong elastic bonds within the dough. The tighter the elastic bonds, the stronger the dough. The amount of protein can vary across all grades of flour, depending on the type of wheat and its growing conditions.

Protein is measured as a percentage of the flour weight. This information is available on most packaging, displayed as protein grams per 100 grams of flour, so,

simply, 12g equals 12% protein. As a quick reference, flour with 13% or more protein is referred to as strong or hard flour, 11% or less referred to as soft or weak flour. A loaf of bread is usually made with strong flour to give it real body and chew, while cakes and pastry are usually made with a softer flour for a more delicate, short texture.

So for the soft and long-rising dough we opt for the very fine 00 flour with a protein content of 12.5%. Just slightly above the medium strength. This is just strong enough to hold all the air as the dough slowly rises, but soft enough to create a light crust. This balanced flour has got our dough off to a great start.

The Original Flour

When pizza first emerged in Naples they probably used something similar to wholewheat flour, but when refined white flour became all the rage at the turn of the 19th century they also started using the finer milled flour to make silky-smooth pizza dough. 00 flour still stands as the traditional choice today in most pizzerias in Naples and around the world, but some are experimenting and evolving the dough with different types and combinations of flours.

Mulino Caputo

At Pizza Pilgrims we specifically use Caputo Blue Pizzeria Flour. We have made the pilgrimage many times to the Caputo mill, to see their flour being made and to marvel at how much intricacy and research goes into sourcing and producing what is some of the best flour in the world. They achieve their own balance, which is a constant activity of adjusting mixes of grains and reacting to fluctuating weather patterns and growth conditions from around the world.

ITALY	UK
2	Wholewheat
1	Plain/All-Purpose
0	Bread Flour
00	Cake Flour

Fig i. **Italian to UK/US flour**

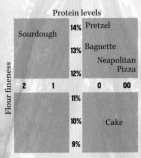

Fig ii. **Typical flour milling and protein levels for baked goods**

WATER

Water, while a seemingly simple ingredient, plays a vital role as the solvent in which the other ingredients are combined and dispersed evenly throughout the dough. It also greatly influences the texture. Not enough water makes the dough stiff and tight. Too much water makes it wet and sticky. To get it just right we use a volume of water equivalent to 62% of the flour weight. In baking terms it's called the dough hydration, and you can apply this percentage to whatever amount of flour you are using to determine the correct amount of water. So for 1000g of flour, we calculate that we would need 620ml water.

Baker Percentages

This is a common method used in baking to calculate the amounts of ingredients. As flour is regarded as the heaviest ingredient, all other ingredients are expressed as a percentage of that total flour weight. This allows recipes to be quickly scaled up and down, or to make accurate adjustments to ingredients. To calculate, we simply divide the weight of the ingredient by the total weight of the flour and multiply by 100:

$$\text{Baker's \%} = \frac{\text{Ingredients}}{\text{Flour Weight}} \times 100$$

Fig iii. **Baker Percentages**

SALT

Salt makes pizza dough taste good. If you imagine flavour is a sound, adding salt would be like turning the volume up loud. In addition, it quietly works on some chemistry in the background by using its preservative qualities to control the rate of fermentation. By slowing things down it gives our dough more time to mature and develop flavour.

Typical bread dough uses about 2% salt (remember our baker percentages), but for Neapolitan pizza we turn the volume up a bit louder and go for 3% salt. Neapolitan pizza is quite thin, so we need maximum taste in the small layer of crust.

Use a good-quality fine sea salt. Try to avoid any table salt or iodised salt as they tend to be processed and not beneficial for flavour.

A Pizzaiolo Never Forgets

You would think it's a fool-proof recipe having very few ingredients; however, they are all absolutely crucial to the dough – without one the dough simply won't work. I learnt this the hard way on my second weekend of our first pizzeria on Dean Street, Soho. That evening something wasn't right. The pizzas were coming out flat, a bit beige and bland, and the customers noticed. The chefs and I checked everything; maybe the dough was too cold? Maybe the oven wasn't hot enough? But when I investigated the dough room in the basement, I found 750g of salt, perfectly measured out, but not in the dough... To this day, I still taste a piece of raw dough after mixing to ensure I remembered the salt.

YEAST

Probably the most fascinating ingredient, yeast is the living element in dough. It's a micro-organism with a sweet tooth. Yeast consumes the sugars from the flour and 'burps' out carbon dioxide. It's this carbon dioxide which swells the gluten network, filling the dough with tiny air bubbles and making it rise.

As the dough expands, yeast also takes part in fermentation. In a very similar process to how beer or wine is made, this fermentation breaks down starches into acids and alcohol, developing all the lovely flavours you get from bread. Time is crucial for this fermentation. Controlling the rate of fermentation is mainly achieved by varying the amount of yeast used as well as the temperature of the dough.

We want to use a very low amount of yeast, to make it work long and hard on fermenting. In the pizzeria we use on average an amount of yeast equivalent to 0.05% of the flour weight. That is 0.5g of yeast for every 1000g of flour. But it doesn't stop there, as yeast is very sensitive to temperature, speeding up in warmer environments and slowing down when it's colder. To counter, we use more yeast when it's colder, and less when it's warmer.

In the summer we may drop the yeast as low as 0.02% and in the winter we may bump it up to near 0.1%.

At home, you're likely using a kilo or two of flour, so measuring anything less than 1g of yeast is going to be pretty difficult. As a standard we recommend using 0.2% yeast which equates to 2g of yeast for every 1000g of flour.

The particular species of yeast for bread baking can be commercially manufactured and is available in 3 forms:

Fresh Yeast

Also known as compressed or cake yeast, is our preferred format here. It's naturally active, easily measured and offers more control on our fermentation rate, making it perfect for a slow rise. It can often be purchased from bakeries or some pizzerias, and is also available in larger supermarkets that have dedicated in-store bakeries – just ask. You can also order online.

Active Dry Yeast

This is a good second choice. It is essentially the same but with moisture removed and ground up into granules. To adjust a recipe to active dry yeast multiply the fresh quantity by 0.4.

Instant Yeast

Also known as fast acting yeast, this is formulated for rapid rising – not exactly suitable for our long fermentation, so avoid if possible. Still, if needs must, to adjust the recipe for instant yeast multiply the fresh quantity by 0.33.

KNEADİNG & MİXİNG

We mix our dough based on the below percentages:

'00' Flour (100%)
Water (62%)
Fine Sea Salt (3%)
Fresh Yeast (0.2%)

In the pizzerias, we have machines to mix our dough, but at home you may be relying on your hands to work the magic. Some may prefer to mix the ingredients in a bowl or dough hook mixer, both of which are great, but we're going to end up kneading by hand on the table top anyway so I prefer to avoid washing up more utensils than needed and just do everything with my hands, traditional style, pretending I'm as authentic or as good as my Neapolitan mates.

Cheffy tip: have all your ingredients measured out before you begin. Measuring each ingredient as you need it isn't fun, and you'll look like a pro as you whip through the recipe with grace.

First the yeast is dissolved in the water. This will help it disperse evenly throughout the dough and ensure it gets maximum exposure to all the starch in the flour. It's crucially important we use tepid water. Remember, yeast is very sensitive to temperature, so do not use warm or ice cold water. Warm water will send the yeast into a frenzy, while ice cold water will shock it frozen, making it inactive. Mixing dough by hand won't heat the dough up much, but if you're using a machine you may need to cool the water to compensate for heat caused by friction. On the other hand, in winter, water from the tap is ice cold and may need warming slightly. Then we slowly introduce the water to the flour. This is where the fun

begins. The starch in the flour swells as it absorbs the water and creates the familiar texture of dough. The proteins bind together and form the strands of gluten. The yeast becomes part of the dough and has access to all the sugars in the flour.

The matter of when to add the salt is fiercely debated among pizza chefs. Some strongly believe that the salt kills the yeast and so it should be added at the end, while others disagree, arguing that they're eventually going to be mixed and spend hours together anyway. We err on the side of caution and add the salt near the end of mixing. It doesn't take much effort, so why not?

Kneading is a vital step for the dough – working the gluten strands into strong networks and creating strength and elasticity. Just like exercising our own muscles, the more we stretch and stress the gluten, the stronger it becomes. It takes around 8–10 minutes to work enough gluten for Neapolitan pizza. More than that and it becomes too tough and firm, so try not to over-knead.

The end result will be a silky-smooth mass of dough. It should be tenacious and elastic, but still soft and relaxed.

FERMENTATİON

Fermentation happens when we allow the yeast enough time to work its magic. Time is crucial here. The more time, the more fermentation. The more fermentation, the more flavour is developed. We allow a lot of time for our dough in the pizzeria, at least 48 hours to be precise, in a process known as double fermentation. However, at home a single overnight fermentation for your dough will still produce a great end product.

Single Fermentation

Divide your dough into individual dough balls: 230g (8oz) for a 10-inch

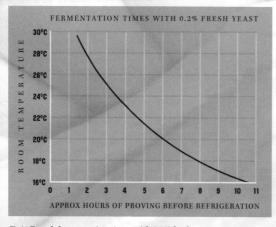

ROOM TEMPERATURE

30°C
28°C
26°C
24°C
22°C
20°C
18°C
16°C

0 1 2 3 4 5 6 7 8 9 10 11

APPROX HOURS OF PROVING BEFORE REFRIGERATION

Fig iv. **Dough fermentation times with 0.2% fresh yeast**

pizza or 260g (9oz) for a 12-inch pizza. Place these in a flat tray or container which you can seal airtight, or cover with clingfilm (plastic wrap). Leave your dough balls to ferment. Ideally place them somewhere with a consistent ambient temperature, as close to 20°C/68°F as possible. Avoid direct sunlight or anywhere with moving air. With our yeast at 0.2% of flour weight it should take approximately 6 hours for the dough to expand to almost double its original size, depending on room temperature. Refer to Fig iv for temperature vs hours for exact timings.

At this point, place the dough balls into the fridge to rest for at least another 18 hours. They can happily remain in the fridge for up to 2 days. It's the extra patience that goes a long way. The dough balls must be brought back to room temperature before making pizza. Cold dough is no good, since the yeast is asleep and the gluten is stiff. We need the yeast to wake up and the gluten to relax before cooking. So remove your dough from the fridge 2 hours before you want to cook it.

Double Fermentation

For those who want to take it to the next level, this method will extend the fermentation even further to maximise flavour. The first fermentation gives the yeast time to access all the starch from the flour and begin breaking it down. The second fermentation then enhances the flavour developed during the first fermentation and shapes the dough in preparation to make pizza.

This time, do not portion the dough into balls immediately. Instead, leave it as a whole or in 'bulk' in a container big enough to allow some expansion. The container must be airtight with a lid or sealed with clingfilm (plastic wrap). Let the dough rest like this overnight at ambient temperature.

The next morning divide your dough into individual

dough balls (see sizing for 'single fermentation'), knocking out the air and reworking each of them back into a tight ball. Place the dough balls in a flat tray or container which you can seal airtight, or cover with clingfilm. Leave these to ferment again for approximately 6 hours for the dough to expand to almost double its original size. Refer to Fig iv for exact timings.

Place them into the fridge to rest at least overnight. They can happily remain in the fridge for up to 2 days. The dough balls must be brought back to room temperature before making pizza. Cold dough is no good, since the yeast is asleep and the gluten is stiff. We need the yeast to wake up and the gluten to relax before cooking. So remove your dough from the fridge 2 hours before you want to cook it. By now, the dough should be at least 48 hours fermented before you make pizza.

Our resident dough man, Mr. Mullin.

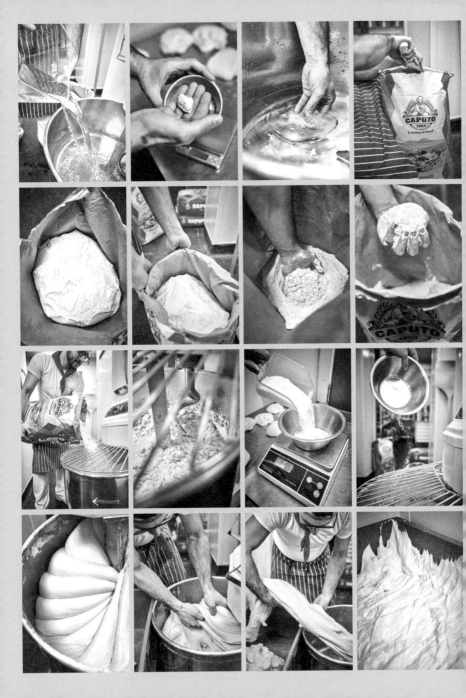

The Recipes

Here it is, our greatest hits of pizza that we have featured on the menu at Pizza Pilgrims. This is basically the culmination of eleven years of obsessing about pizza. Enjoy!

MAKING NEAPOLITAN PIZZA DOUGH

With the knowledge of each ingredient and the important roles they play, we can now make Neapolitan pizza dough.

Tip: Weigh out all your ingredients before you start.

Makes: enough for 6–7 10-inch pizzas.

INGREDIENTS

1000g (35oz) '00' flour
(we recommend Caputo 'blue')

2g (⅔tsp) fresh yeast

620ml (21fl oz) tepid water

30g (1oz) fine sea salt

METHOD

1. Make a mountain of flour in the middle of the table. Using your fist, make a deep well in the middle of the flour, exposing the surface of the table (turning your mountain into a moon crater).

2. Crumble the yeast into the tepid water. Use your good hand to mash up the yeast in the water until it has dissolved. (Keep the other hand dry for taking Instagram photos to show off to your friends.) Fill your crater of flour with a third of the yeast/water mix. Using your fingertips, start making very small circular motions to combine the flour and water.

3. Start dragging in some more flour to the mix, by 'undercutting' the walls of the crater with your fingertips. As you do this the mixture in the middle will become thicker. Once it reaches the consistency of porridge you need to add a bit more water. Don't let it get too thick; if it starts to form a dough too soon it becomes difficult to incorporate the rest of the water. Keep dragging in a little flour to thicken the mix, then pouring a little bit more water in to loosen it, until you have used up all the water.

4. Sprinkle the sea salt over the mixture while it's still very wet to ensure it dissolves and disperses evenly throughout the dough. Now use both hands to push the remaining flour from the outside into the middle. Fold and press the mix until all the flour is absorbed and a dough comes together. If you have a dough scraper it really helps get everything off the table, but you can improvise with a paint scraper, spatula or knife.

5. Work the gluten by kneading the dough. Use the heel of your hand to stretch out the dough and roll it back up, while the other hand acts like an anchor. You'll be able to see the strands of gluten stretching, breaking, being put back together and becoming stronger. Continue this for about 8 minutes until the dough becomes smooth and glossy. It should also feel tighter and elastic.

6. Let the dough have a 10-minute rest to relax the gluten. Cover the dough with a damp cloth or some clingfilm (plastic wrap) to keep the air from drying it out. Then divide your bulk of dough into 6–7 individual portions. We recommend 230g (8oz) dough balls for 10-inch pizzas. Ensure your dough balls are neatly shaped – pinched at the bottom and tight on the top – then place them in a tray or container 3cm (1in) apart. Cover with a tight lid or clingfilm (plastic wrap).

7. Now you can relax. The yeast will take over from here. Leave the dough at room temperature for approximately 6 hours until it expands to almost double its size, then store in the fridge overnight. The next day remove the dough from the fridge for 1–2 hours and bring it back to room temperature before making your pizzas.

STRETCHING YOUR OWN PIZZA BASE

Want to look like a boss when making pizza at home? That's what we thought. This is the traditional Neapolitan technique, in which you *have* to use your hands (a rolling pin is an absolute no-no). So, roll up your sleeves, dust your hands with flour like a gymnast stepping up to the parallel bars and channel your inner *pizzaiolo*.

1. Place your dough ball on a lightly floured surface then generously dust with more '00' flour. The dough ball should be completely covered in flour, as you don't want any sticky spots.

2. Using your fingertips, press out the dough ball firmly, starting at the centre and working your way out to the edges. It's important that this motion is a 'push down' and not a 'stretch out'. As you push out to the edges, leave the last inch of the dough untouched. This will become your crust.

3. Turn the dough over and repeat the process. The aim is to end up with a circle of dough about half the size of the final pizza, with a thin middle and a raised crust.

4. Transfer the pizza base to the back of your hands. The edge of the crust should rest on your knuckles, with the rest of the base hanging down. (It's a good idea to 'de-bling' just before this stage, as jewellery will poke a hole in the delicate dough.)

5. Now start stretching the dough between your hands. Try to stretch the outside edge, rather than the centre, as it will become too thin. Keep rotating the pizza base until you have arrived back where you started. Now you should have a 10-inch (ish) pizza base with a raised crust and a beautifully thin middle. If you hold it up to a light you should almost be able to see through it.

Fixing holes

If you over-stretch your dough and it gets too thin, you can end up with little holes in your pizza base. Just squeeze these back together before you put any toppings on. Easy.

Stuck pizzas

Try to move quickly with the dough, as it can stick to the work surface if left too long. If you're generous with the flour and add more during the process, you shouldn't end up in a sticky situation.

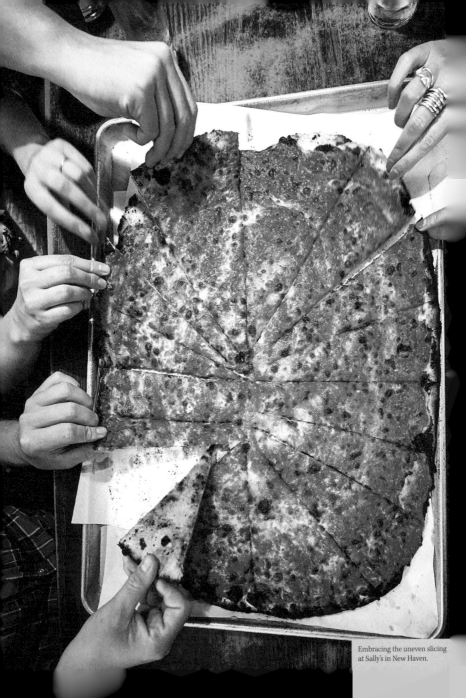

Embracing the uneven slicing at Sally's in New Haven.

FRYING PAN PIZZA

We totally believe that making pizza using our frying pan (skillet) pizza method makes for the absolute best Neapolitan pizza you can make at home. Follow these simple steps below and we're sure you'll agree with us.

Turn on your grill (broiler) to its highest setting and place an ovenproof frying pan (skillet) over a high heat. Grab your dough.

Stretch out the pizza base following the instructions on page 37.

Once your pizza base is about 10 inches wide, lay it in the hot, dry frying pan.

Add the tomato sauce, Parmesan, basil, mozzarella and olive oil (in that order).

When the base of the pizza has some colour and the crust has risen slightly, put the pan on the highest shelf under the hot grill.

When the crust has tuned slightly golden and it has some good char bubbles your pizza is ready to eat!

TOP TIPS

- Before you start, place your frying pan (skillet) on the heat, turn your grill (broiler) on and place your oven shelf on the top rung – the hotter the better with this method.

- Use a wide-based ovenproof frying pan (skillet). Please don't melt any plastic handles!
- The olive oil goes on the pizza – not in the pan!

Margherita

Where pizza all began... we can still remember the first time we tried a proper Neapolitan Margherita in Da Michele in Naples while on our Pizza Pilgrimage. The mozzarella had been made that day and was perfect. The combination of the light, charred pizza dough, sweet tomatoes, aromatic basil, peppery olive oil, savoury Parmesan and the milky white, creamy and slightly acidic mozzarella, just creates the most perfect flavour balance, which is the reason that the Margherita is the undisputed heavyweight champion of pizza. It is always the pizza that any pizza chef would order to get the measure of a new pizzeria because there is nothing to hide behind; no snazzy flavours to mask the quality of your ingredients, dough and skill in the oven.

FOR THE TOMATO SAUCE

Makes enough for 4 pizzas
1 x 400g (14oz) can of San Marzano (or any good-quality Italian) tomatoes
a good pinch of sea salt

METHOD

In a large bowl, crush the tomatoes by hand. (This is the old-school way they used to do it in Naples, and for good reason. If you put the tomatoes in a food processor you end up with a depressingly smooth sauce that lacks texture.) Once you've crushed the hell out of your tomatoes, add a pinch of salt to taste and that's it! Pure, unadulterated tomato goodness.

FOR THE PİZZA

1 ball of Neapolitan pizza dough (see page 36)
80g (3oz) tomato sauce (see left)
4–5 fresh basil leaves
Parmesan, for grating
1 tbsp olive oil
80g (3oz) fior di latte mozzarella, torn or sliced

METHOD

1. Preheat the grill (broiler) to its absolute highest setting, and place a large, ovenproof frying pan (skillet) over a high heat and let it get screaming hot.

2. Meanwhile, flatten and stretch the dough ball (following the instructions on page 37) to make a 10-inch pizza base.

3. Lay the pizza base flat in the hot, dry frying pan, then, using a small ladle (or a large spoon), spoon the tomato sauce onto the middle of the pizza. Using the back of the ladle, make concentric circles to spread the sauce, beginning in the middle and finishing 1½in from the edge.

4. Next, sprinkle over the basil (it will burn if put on last). Grate over a little Parmesan and drizzle with the olive oil.

5. Once the base of the pizza has browned, about 1–2 minutes, add your mozzarella, then place the frying pan under the grill on the highest shelf.

6. Once the crust has taken on some colour, about 1–2 minutes, the pizza is ready!

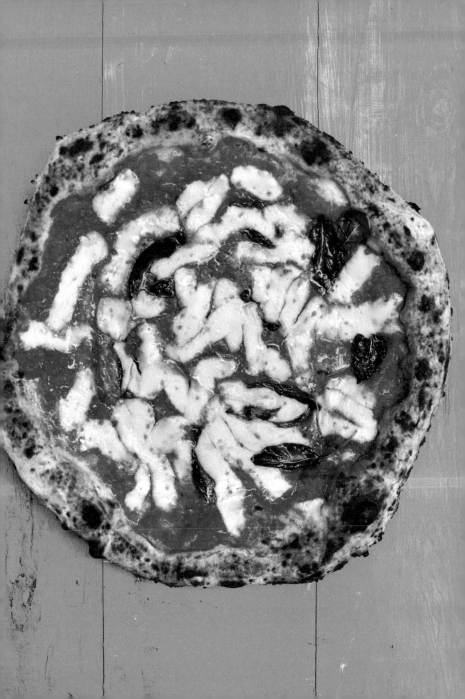

Marinara

The Marinara precedes even the Margherita. It's so called because it was the dish that was cooked for the fishermen of Naples when they came in off the boats.

They did not have a lot of money to spend on food, so this flatbread topped with local tomatoes, garlic, olive oil and dried oregano became a local favourite. For us, the Marinara is the definition of 'punching above its weight' because, to be fair, it does at first glance look like a slightly naked Margherita. Do not underestimate the combo of garlic and herbs, though, because as soon as you take a bite you are smacked with a huge flavour punch. When this pizza is made right, it is pretty hard to beat.

INGREDIENTS

1 ball of Neapolitan pizza dough (see page 36)

140g (5oz) tomato sauce (see page 42)

½ garlic clove, finely sliced

1 tbsp good-quality olive oil

4–5 basil leaves

a good pinch of dried oregano

METHOD

1. Preheat the grill (broiler) to its absolute highest setting, and place a large, ovenproof frying pan (skillet) over a high heat and let it get screaming hot.

2. Meanwhile, flatten and stretch the dough ball (following the instructions on page 37) to make a 10-inch pizza base.

3. Lay the pizza base flat in the hot, dry frying pan, then, using a small ladle (or a large spoon), spoon the tomato sauce onto the middle of the pizza. Using the back of the ladle, make concentric circles to spread the sauce, beginning in the middle and finishing 1½in from the edge.

4. Top the pizza with the garlic slices, olive oil and basil. Once the base of the pizza has browned, about 1–2 minutes, place the frying pan under the grill on the highest shelf.

5. Once the crust has taken on some colour, about 1–2 minutes, remove the pizza from the grill and sprinkle with the dried oregano.

Bufala

The only thing cooler than ordering a Margherita in a Neapolitan pizzeria is ordering a bufala (and preferably adopting a strong Italian accent while wildly gesticulating with your hands – go on try it now... makes you feel good, right?). Neapolitans are intensely proud of their fior di latte, but the Mozzarella Di Bufala Campana is both DOC and DOP protected in Italy (essentially the more acronyms a product has after its name the posher it is – a lot like people, really). The mozzarella made using the milk from water buffalo has a higher fat content and therefore more flavour. We prefer to tear buffalo mozzarella instead of slicing it, as it keeps more of the milk in the cheese. The only real debate is whether it should be added before or after the pizza is cooked. Before means you get a beautiful melty stretch to the mozzarella, but after protects more of its delicate milkiness. Or just do what we do, and do both...

INGREDIENTS

1 ball of Neapolitan pizza dough (see page 36)

80g (3oz) tomato sauce (see page 42)

4–5 basil leaves

Parmesan, for grating

1 tbsp good-quality olive oil

80g (3oz) buffalo mozzarella, torn into pieces

METHOD

1. Preheat the grill (broiler) to its absolute highest setting, and place a large, ovenproof frying pan (skillet) over a high heat and let it get screaming hot.

2. Meanwhile, flatten and stretch the dough ball (following the instructions on page 37) to make a 10-inch pizza base.

3. Lay the pizza base flat in the hot, dry frying pan, then, using a small ladle (or a large spoon), spoon the tomato sauce onto the middle of the pizza. Using the back of the ladle, make concentric circles to spread the sauce, beginning in the middle and finishing 1½in from the edge. Then add the basil, a grating of Parmesan and the olive oil.

4. Once the base of the pizza has browned, about 1–2 minutes, add the mozzarella, then place the frying pan under the grill on the highest shelf for 1–2 minutes until the crust has taken on some colour. Or, make the pizza more like a Marinara (page 44) then top with cold, fresh buffalo mozzarella. (Or do both!)

Double Pepperoni & Spicy Honey

Spicy honey on pizza is an idea that we borrowed from our good friend Paulie Gee, of Paulie Gee's pizzeria in Greenpoint, NYC. Along with his first head chef, Mike, he created the Hellboy, a Marg topped with sopressata picante sausage and hot honey made by Mike. Mike ended up moving on from Paulie Gee's and starting Mike's Hot Honey, which is hands down the best spicy honey there is. We took this idea and put our own spin on it by adding two different types of pepperoni. We tried to import Mike's honey from the US but, after two failed attempts in which cases of honey got incinerated at customs (don't ask), we decided to create our own.

INGREDIENTS

1 ball of Neapolitan pizza dough
(see page 36)

80g (3oz) tomato sauce (see page 42)

4–5 basil leaves

Parmesan, for grating

1 tbsp good-quality olive oil

30g (1oz) each of 2 different types of sliced pepperoni

1 fresh chilli, sliced

80g (3oz) fior di latte mozzarella, torn or sliced

FOR THE SPICY HONEY

Makes enough for 10 pizzas

40g (1½oz) fresh chilli, sliced

100ml (scant ½ cup/3½fl oz) honey

METHOD

1. First, make the spicy honey by adding the chilli to the honey and leaving it to develop (at least 12 hours, but it keeps for up to 3 weeks).

2. Preheat the grill (broiler) to its absolute highest setting, and place a large, ovenproof frying pan (skillet) over a high heat and let it get screaming hot.

3. Meanwhile, flatten and stretch the dough ball (following the instructions on page 37) to make a 10-inch pizza base.

4. Lay the pizza base flat in the hot, dry frying pan, then, using a small ladle (or a large spoon), spoon the tomato sauce onto the middle of the pizza. Using the back of the ladle, make concentric circles to spread the sauce, beginning in the middle and finishing 1½in from the edge. Then add the basil, a grating of Parmesan, the olive oil, pepperoni and fresh chilli.

5. Once the base of the pizza has browned, about 1–2 minutes, add the mozzarella, then place the frying pan under the grill on the highest shelf.

6. Once the crust has taken on some colour, about 1–2 minutes, drizzle with some spicy honey and eat.

Smoked Napoli

This pizza still confuses us but we love it. It essentially involves putting all the saltiest ingredients on one pizza! We don't really understand how but the result is not overly salty. It's magic really. We use meaty smoked anchovies in oil that have a deep flavour, but you can use regular anchovy fillets if you like. Try to find tiny Lilliput capers that pop in your mouth, and the tiny purple olives that have a great savouriness to them. This is probably the most divisive pizza on our menu but also has the most loyal fans. ALWAYS drink with ice-cold beer.

INGREDIENTS

1 ball of Neapolitan pizza dough (see page 36)

80g (3oz) tomato sauce (see page 42)

4–5 basil leaves

Parmesan, for grating

1 tbsp good-quality olive oil

3 smoked anchovy fillets

1 tsp capers

9 pitted black olives

80g (3oz) fior di latte mozzarella, torn or sliced

a good pinch of dried oregano

METHOD

1. Preheat the grill (broiler) to its absolute highest setting, and place a large, ovenproof frying pan (skillet) over a high heat and let it get screaming hot.

2. Meanwhile, flatten and stretch the dough ball (following the instructions on page 37) to make a 10-inch pizza base.

3. Lay the pizza base flat in the hot, dry frying pan, then, using a small ladle (or a large spoon), spoon the tomato sauce onto the middle of the pizza. Using the back of the ladle, make concentric circles to spread the sauce, beginning in the middle and finishing 1½in from the edge, then add the basil, a grating of Parmesan and the olive oil. Split the anchovy fillets lengthways with your fingers and drape over the pizza, then top with the capers and olives.

4. Once the base of the pizza has browned, about 1–2 minutes, add the mozzarella, then place the frying pan under the grill on the highest shelf.

5. Once the crust has taken on some colour, about 1–2 minutes, sprinkle with the dried oregano and eat.

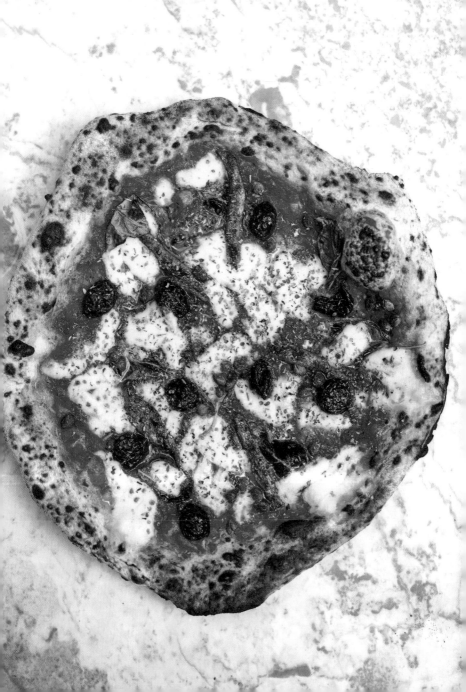

Neapolitan Salami & Fire-roasted Peppers

Neapolitan salami is quite specific when it comes to pizza. It has to have a coarse grain to it, whole black peppercorns in it, and it must be cut into matchsticks, not slices. This massively increases the surface area and means you get more flavour from less salami. We pair the salty salami with sweet, fire-roasted bell peppers.

INGREDIENTS

60g (2oz) Napoli black pepper salami

1 ball of Neapolitan pizza dough
(see page 36)

80g (3oz) tomato sauce (see page 42)

4–5 basil leaves

Parmesan, for grating

1 tbsp good-quality olive oil

40g (1½oz) roasted bell peppers (either jarred or roasted whole over the hob at home)

80g (3oz) fior di latte mozzarella, torn or sliced

METHOD

1. To prepare your salami, cut into slices 3–4mm (⅙–⅛in) thick, then stack the slices like coins and slice into 3–4mm (⅙–⅛in) matchsticks.

2. Preheat the grill (broiler) to its absolute highest setting, and place a large, ovenproof frying pan (skillet) over a high heat and let it get screaming hot.

3. Meanwhile, flatten and stretch the dough ball (following the instructions on page 37) to make a 10-inch pizza base.

4. Lay the pizza base flat in the hot, dry frying pan, then, using a small ladle (or a large spoon), spoon the tomato sauce onto the middle of the pizza. Using the back of the ladle, make concentric circles to spread the sauce, beginning in the middle and finishing 1½in from the edge, then add the basil, a grating of Parmesan and the olive oil. Tear your roasted peppers into bite-sized chunks and place evenly over the pizza, then top with the salami matchsticks.

5. Once the base of the pizza has browned, about 1–2 minutes, add the mozzarella, then place the frying pan under the grill on the highest shelf.

6. Once the crust has taken on some colour, about 1–2 minutes, your pizza is ready!

Aubergine Parmigiana

We wanted a pizza on the menu that would be both vegetarian and a real comfort food hit. The one dish that makes all our pizzaioli go weak at the knees, except pizza, is aubergine parmigiana. So, we put it on a pizza.

FOR THE PARMİGİANA

Makes enough for 5 pizzas

2 aubergines (eggplant), cut into 2cm/¾in cubes

3 garlic cloves, finely chopped

100ml (scant ½ cup) good-quality olive oil

50g (1¾oz) tomato paste

2 x 400g (14oz) cans good-quality peeled plum tomatoes

100ml (scant ½ cup) water

a small handful of basil leaves

salt and freshly ground black pepper

FOR THE PİZZA

1 ball of Neapolitan pizza dough (see page 36)

4–5 basil leaves

Parmesan, for grating, plus 5g (⅛oz) shavings to finish

1 tbsp good-quality olive oil, plus extra for drizzling

25g (1oz) cherry plum tomatoes

80g (3oz) fior di latte mozzarella, torn or sliced

METHOD

1. First, toss the aubergine cubes in salt in a colander set over a bowl and leave for at least an hour. Preheat your oven to 250°C/480°F/ Gas 10.

2. Add your garlic and olive oil to a large, ovenproof saucepan and place over a medium heat. Slowly cook until the garlic is golden brown.

3. Dry the aubergine cubes with a clean cloth, then add them to the pan and cook until the aubergine has softened.

4. Stir in the tomato paste and cook for a further 3 minutes, then add the canned tomatoes and water. Place in the hot oven (with the lid off), stirring occasionally for 30–40 minutes until the sauce has reduced and the aubergine is soft and tender. Season with salt and pepper to taste and leave to cool.

5. Preheat the grill (broiler) to its absolute highest setting, and place a large, ovenproof frying pan (skillet) over a high heat and let it get screaming hot.

6. Meanwhile, flatten and stretch the dough ball (following the instructions on page 37) to make a 10-inch pizza base.

7. Lay the pizza base flat in the hot, dry frying pan, then spread over 100g (3½oz) of the aubergine parmigiana. Top with the basil, a grating of Parmesan, the tablespoon of olive oil and cherry tomatoes.

8. Once the base of the pizza has browned, about 1–2 minutes, add the mozzarella, then place the frying pan under the grill on the highest shelf.

9. Once the crust has taken on some colour, about 1–2 minutes, finish the cooked pizza with the Parmesan shavings and a drizzle of olive oil.

Salsiccia e Friarielli

Things that Neapolitan chefs treasure: Maradona, good espresso, Nutella, their mums... and *salsiccia e friarielli*. This is one of the true flavours of a Naples kitchen. On the face of it, it's just two ingredients: coarse-ground Italian pork sausage and a special type of local wild broccoli called *friarielli*, which is fried in olive oil, garlic and chilli. It can be served as antipasti, or mixed into pasta or risotto. The best way to eat it, though, is on pizza.

FOR THE SALSICCIA E FRIARIELLI

Makes enough for 5 pizzas

olive oil, for cooking

6 big fat Italian pork sausages

2 large garlic cloves, finely sliced

a good pinch of chilli flakes

400g (14oz) fresh or frozen friarielli (use tenderstem broccoli if you can't find it)

a splash of white wine

salt and freshly ground black pepper

METHOD

1. Place a deep frying pan on a medium heat and add a glug of olive oil. Add the whole sausages into the pan and fry for about 5 minutes, until they take on some colour.

2. Add your garlic and chilli flakes and fry for a further 30 seconds, then add your friarielli.

3. Add the wine and simmer for 10–15 minutes until the wine has cooked off, the friarielli is tender and the sausages are cooked all the way through. Remove from the heat, season to taste and set aside to cool. When cool, remove the sausages and cut into chunks.

FOR THE PIZZA

1 ball of Neapolitan pizza dough (see page 36)

155g (5½oz) salsiccia e friarielli (see left)

Parmesan, for grating

1 tbsp good-quality olive oil

sliced fresh chilli, to taste

80g (3oz) smoked mozzarella, torn or sliced

METHOD

1. Preheat the grill (broiler) to its absolute highest setting, and place a large, ovenproof frying pan (skillet) over a high heat and let it get screaming hot.

2. Meanwhile, flatten and stretch the dough ball (following the instructions on page 37) to make a 10-inch pizza base.

3. Lay the pizza base flat in the hot, dry frying pan, then spread the salsiccia e friarielli evenly across the base. Grate over some Parmesan, drizzle over a little olive oil and scatter on the fresh chilli slices.

4. Once the base of the pizza has browned, about 1–2 minutes, add the smoked mozzarella, then place the frying pan under the grill on the highest shelf.

5. Once the crust has taken on some colour, about 1–2 minutes, your pizza is ready!

'Nduja

We are writing this page from Calabria, the home of 'nduja, having just returned from visiting our 'nduja supplier, Vincenzo, who showed us around his factory. The passion for 'nduja in Calabria is huge. It's a style of pork sausage which is made from the fattiest parts of the pig: the cheeks and the belly. The meat is minced finely with salt, Calabrian chillies and a mix of herbs and spices, including fennel and black pepper. It is then kneaded like dough to create an amazing paste which is unceremoniously stuffed into a pig's intestine. From there, the sausage is smoked and cured to mature the flavour. The result is a soft, cured paste that is packed with flavour and fiery heat. Used as a pizza topping it is an absolute winner.

INGREDIENTS

1 ball of Neapolitan pizza dough (see page 36)

80g (3oz) tomato sauce (see page 42)

4–5 basil leaves

Parmesan, for grating

1 tbsp good-quality olive oil

60g (2oz) 'nduja sausage

80g (3oz) fior di latte mozzarella, torn or sliced

METHOD

1. Preheat the grill (broiler) to its absolute highest setting, and place a large, ovenproof frying pan (skillet) over a high heat and let it get screaming hot.

2. Meanwhile, flatten and stretch the dough ball (following the instructions on page 37) to make a 10-inch pizza base.

3. Lay the pizza base flat in the hot, dry frying pan, then, using a small ladle (or a large spoon), spoon the tomato sauce onto the middle of the pizza. Using the back of the ladle, make concentric circles to spread the sauce, beginning in the middle and finishing 1½in from the edge. Then add the basil, a grating of Parmesan and the olive oil. Pinch off pieces of the 'nduja and scatter over the pizza.

4. Once the base of the pizza has browned, about 1–2 minutes, add the mozzarella, then place the frying pan under the grill on the highest shelf.

5. Once the crust has taken on some colour, about 1–2 minutes, your pizza is ready!

Carbonara

We wanted to pay homage to this pasta heavy-hitter by creating its pizza cousin. Carbonara pizza had been done before but in a very anglicised way, with cream and cooked ham... We wanted to stay true to the authentic traditions, which means using guanciale (cured pig's cheek) and, of course, NO cream! As mentioned in Divisive Ingredients, this pizza caused some scandal with our customers. Pasta on pizza is a pizza purist's no-no, but we found ourselves between a rock and hard place – be authentic to carbonara pasta or be authentic to pizza. It really came down to tasting, and carbonara pizza with bucatini pasta on top is *definitely* better... but we do offer it with no pasta to keep everyone happy.

INGREDIENTS

1 ball of Neapolitan pizza dough (see page 36)

50g (1¾oz) cooked and cooled bucatini pasta

Parmesan, for grating

80g (3oz) fior di latte mozzarella, torn or sliced

60g (2oz) diced guanciale (or pancetta if easier), cooked until golden

1 tbsp good-quality olive oil

1 egg yolk, broken up with a fork

freshly ground black pepper

METHOD

1. Preheat the grill (broiler) to its absolute highest setting, and place a large, ovenproof frying pan (skillet) over a high heat and let it get screaming hot.

2. Meanwhile, flatten and stretch the dough ball (following the instructions on page 37) to make a 10-inch pizza base.

3. Lay the pizza base flat in the hot, dry frying pan then drape over the pasta (reserving a few strands). Top with a grating of Parmesan, the mozzarella, guanciale and the olive oil. Add a few more strands of pasta, then drizzle the whole pizza with the egg yolk.

4. Once the base of the pizza has browned, about 1–2 minutes, place the frying pan under the grill on the highest shelf.

5. Once the crust has taken on some colour, about 1–2 minutes, generously season with lots of black pepper and eat.

Roast Mushroom & Truffle

One of the great Italian flavour combinations, mushroom and truffle were made for each other. We used to serve this pizza simply using thinly sliced mushrooms, like most pizzerias. But we wanted a deeper mushroom flavour so we developed a technique of roasting the sliced mushrooms in the oven with olive oil, garlic, pepper and salt. Lots of mushroom liquor, which is full of flavour, runs out of the mushrooms so we use a little flour to thicken the liquid to create an intensely flavourful mushroom ragu that we spoon over the base. Once cooked, we top it with a drizzle of white truffle oil from Alba.

INGREDIENTS

1 ball of Neapolitan pizza dough
(see page 36)

4–5 basil leaves

Parmesan, for grating

1 tbsp good-quality olive oil

80g (3oz) fior di latte mozzarella, torn or sliced

1 tbsp white truffle oil

FOR THE MUSHROOM MIXTURE

Makes enough for 4 pizzas

100ml (scant ½ cup) good-quality olive oil

4 garlic cloves, finely chopped

500g (1lb 2oz) chestnut mushrooms, finely sliced

a good pinch of salt

1 tbsp plain (all-purpose) flour

METHOD

1. First make the mushroom mixture by heating the olive oil and garlic gently in a saucepan. Allow the garlic to turn golden before adding the sliced mushrooms and salt. Fry until the mushrooms have softened and their liquid has been released.

2. Take off the heat, tilt the mushrooms to one side of the pan and collect the mushroom juices in the other side of the pan. Stir the flour into the liquid until smooth and put back on the heat. Stir continuously until you have a thick liquor coating the mushrooms. Leave to cool.

3. Preheat the grill (broiler) to its absolute highest setting, and place a large, ovenproof frying pan (skillet) over a high heat and let it get screaming hot.

4. Meanwhile, flatten and stretch the dough ball (following the instructions on page 37) to make a 10-inch pizza base.

5. Lay the pizza base flat in the hot, dry frying pan, then spread with some mushroom mixture. Top with the basil, a grating of Parmesan and the olive oil.

6. Once the base of the pizza has browned, about 1–2 minutes, add the mozzarella, then place the frying pan under the grill on the highest shelf.

7. Once the crust has taken on some colour, about 1–2 minutes, drizzle with the truffle oil and eat.

Capricciosa

The translation of the word capricciosa tells you everything you need to know about this pizza and why it is such a menu staple; the word directly translates as 'capricious', which the Oxford dictionary defines as: 'Given to sudden and unaccountable changes of mood and behaviour'. Amazing. Who doesn't know a fickle pizza orderer who incessantly claims, 'I don't know what to have!'? This pizza solves that problem because it is basically topped with every ingredient in the pizzaiolo's arsenal. You can order this pizza safe in the knowledge that you will not experience pizza FOMO or orderer's remorse.

INGREDIENTS

1 ball of Neapolitan pizza dough
(see page 36)

80g (3oz) tomato sauce (see page 42)

4–5 basil leaves

Parmesan, for grating

1 tbsp good-quality olive oil

35g (1¼oz) chargrilled artichokes
(in oil, from a jar)

50g (1¾oz) prosciutto cotto

40g (1½oz) mushroom mixture (see page 62)

30g (1oz) black olives

80g (3oz) fior di latte mozzarella, torn or sliced

a good pinch of dried oregano

METHOD

1. Preheat the grill (broiler) to its absolute highest setting, and place a large, ovenproof frying pan (skillet) over a high heat and let it get screaming hot.

2. Meanwhile, flatten and stretch the dough ball (following the instructions on page 37) to make a 10-inch pizza base.

3. Lay the pizza base flat in the hot, dry frying pan, then, using a small ladle (or a large spoon), spoon the tomato sauce onto the middle of the pizza. Using the back of the ladle, make concentric circles to spread the sauce, beginning in the middle and finishing 1½in from the edge. Then add the basil, a grating of Parmesan and the olive oil. Top with the artichokes, prosciutto cotto, mushroom mixture and olives.

4. Once the base of the pizza has browned, about 1–2 minutes, add the mozzarella, then place the frying pan under the grill on the highest shelf.

5. Once the crust has taken on some colour, about 1–2 minutes, scatter with dried oregano and eat.

Fiorentina

It was actually the French who first coined the phrase *a la Florentine*, to describe dishes featuring spinach, cheese and egg. It's not known why, but eggs Florentine is a breakfast staple the world over. With that logic it can be deduced that pizza fiorentina is a perfect breakfast pizza to be eaten without shame or guilt (although all pizzas are breakfast pizzas, right?). Our version of this green goddess of a pizza was developed by our very own head chef Tom Mullin, a Northern Irish lad with a penchant for good Irish butter.

INGREDIENTS

a large knob of butter

200g (7oz) spinach leaves, finely shredded

80g (3oz) double (heavy) cream

¼ tsp freshly grated nutmeg

Parmesan, for grating

1 ball of Neapolitan pizza dough
(see page 36)

80g (3oz) fior di latte mozzarella, torn or sliced

1 egg yolk

sea salt and cracked black pepper

METHOD

1. First melt the knob of butter in a pan, then fill the pan with the spinach. Wait until it has wilted down then add the cream, nutmeg, and some salt and pepper to taste. Cook down for a few minutes, remove from the heat and grate in some Parmesan to taste. Leave to cool.

2. Preheat the grill (broiler) to its absolute highest setting, and place a large, ovenproof frying pan (skillet) over a high heat and let it get screaming hot.

3. Meanwhile, flatten and stretch the dough ball (following the instructions on page 37) to make a 10-inch pizza base.

4. Lay the pizza base flat in the hot, dry frying pan, then spread with the spinach mixture. Add the mozzarella and some more grated Parmesan, then gently place the egg yolk in the centre of the pizza.

5. Once the base of the pizza has browned, about 1–2 minutes, place the frying pan under the grill on the highest shelf.

6. Once the crust has taken on some colour, about 1–2 minutes, finish with some cracked black pepper.

Americano

In the years following World War II there was a wave of Americanisation that swept across southern Italy. It was immortalised in the 1956 jazz hit *Tu Vuò Fà L'Americano* ('You want to be an American'), which sung about a Neapolitan man who wanted to live like an American, drinking whisky and soda, dancing to rock and roll, playing baseball and smoking Camel cigarettes. This pizza is an ode to the love of American culture and has a place in the traditional Neapolitan pizza line-up. An absolute favourite among kids, the pizza is essentially a Margherita topped with French fries and sliced-up Frankfurters. In short: It. Is. Delicious. But it is not one your doctor would like you eating.

INGREDIENTS

1 ball of Neapolitan pizza dough
(see page 36)

80g (3oz) tomato sauce (see page 42)

4–5 basil leaves

Parmesan, for grating

1 tbsp good-quality olive oil

60g (2oz) Frankfurter sausage, sliced

80g (3oz) fior di latte mozzarella, torn or sliced

80g (3oz) cooked fries

tomato ketchup, to serve

METHOD

1. Preheat the grill (broiler) to its absolute highest setting, and place a large, ovenproof frying pan (skillet) over a high heat and let it get screaming hot.

2. Meanwhile, flatten and stretch the dough ball (following the instructions on page 37) to make a 10-inch pizza base.

3. Lay the pizza base flat in the hot, dry frying pan, then, using a small ladle (or a large spoon), spoon the tomato sauce onto the middle of the pizza. Using the back of the ladle, make concentric circles to spread the sauce, beginning in the middle and finishing 1½in from the edge. Then add the basil, a grating of Parmesan, the olive oil and the sliced Frankfurter sausage.

4. Once the base of the pizza has browned, about 1–2 minutes, add the mozzarella, then place the frying pan under the grill on the highest shelf.

5. Once the crust has taken on some colour, about 1–2 minutes, scatter the fries over the top and serve with ketchup.

Datterini Filetti

The celebration of tomatoes, mozzarella and basil on a pizza is where it all began, and this pizza makes a slight twist on the Margherita, with dramatic effect. By switching out the pulped San Marzano tomato for little sliced datterini tomatoes you completely change the flavour of the pizza. The tomatoes have a sweet acidity that you don't get in a tomato sauce, and when you bite into them, they pop, giving you an explosion of tomato flavour. This is the ultimate summer pizza, and feels light and refreshing like a tomato salad. To take this pizza to the next level, top with a whole burrata before serving. Naughty.

INGREDIENTS

1 ball of Neapolitan pizza dough (see page 36)

80g (3oz) pesto

4–5 basil leaves

Parmesan, for grating

1 tbsp good-quality olive oil, plus extra to finish

80g (3oz) baby datterini tomatoes, sliced

a pinch of salt

80g (3oz) fior di latte mozzarella, torn or sliced

whole burrata (optional)

METHOD

1. Preheat the grill (broiler) to its absolute highest setting, and place a large, ovenproof frying pan (skillet) over a high heat and let it get screaming hot.

2. Meanwhile, flatten and stretch the dough ball (following the instructions on page 37) to make a 10-inch pizza base.

3. Lay the pizza base flat in the hot, dry frying pan, then spread with the pesto. Next add the basil, a grating of Parmesan and the olive oil.

4. Toss the sliced tomatoes in a pinch of salt.

5. Once the base of the pizza has browned, about 1–2 minutes, add the mozzarella and tomatoes, then place the frying pan under the grill on the highest shelf.

6. Once the crust has taken on some colour, about 1–2 minutes, top with a whole burrata (if using) and drizzle with some more olive oil.

Gianfranco GorgonZola

This was a rare opportunity to celebrate two things that we love: creamy Gorgonzola blue cheese from Milan and the Italian football legend and nineties star of London's Chelsea Football Club, Gianfranco Zola. Much like its namesake, this pizza has an explosive energy, great strength and an understanding of the offside rule that is unrivalled (hang on – this analogy is beginning to fall over...). Truth be told, it's just a great pun but is nonetheless a delicious pizza. We pair this with an Italian wheat beer, and it's a hell of a combo.

INGREDIENTS

1 small courgette (zucchini)

1 ball of Neapolitan pizza dough (see page 36)

4–5 basil leaves

60g (2oz) sweet Gorgonzola, in small pieces

Parmesan, for grating

1 tbsp good-quality olive oil

80g (3oz) fior di latte mozzarella, torn or sliced

a good pinch of dried oregano

METHOD

1. Using a speed/swivel peeler, create courgette ribbons by running the peeler lengthways down the courgette. You need about 50g (1¾oz).

2. Preheat the grill (broiler) to its absolute highest setting, and place a large, ovenproof frying pan (skillet) over a high heat and let it get screaming hot.

3. Meanwhile, flatten and stretch the dough ball (following the instructions on page 37) to make a 10-inch pizza base.

4. Lay the pizza base flat in the hot, dry frying pan, then scatter over the basil leaves and courgette ribbons. Top with the Gorgonzola, a grating of Parmesan and the olive oil.

5. Once the base of the pizza has browned, about 1–2 minutes, add the mozzarella, then place the frying pan under the grill on the highest shelf.

6. Once the crust has taken on some colour, about 1–2 minutes, scatter with some dried oregano and eat.

Mimosa

Another favourite of the kids of Naples, everything about this pizza screams comfort. Think of it like the Neapolitan equivalent of the British fish fingers, chips and baked beans supper. The mimosa is actually a little yellow flower which is given to women on International Women's Day. We serve this pizza each March to celebrate the female pizzaiolas in our company and IWD. The Italians flock to buy it but, oddly, Londoners tend to turn their nose up at it (they are missing out!).

INGREDIENTS

1 ball of Neapolitan pizza dough (see page 36)

40ml (1¼fl oz) double (heavy) cream

4–5 basil leaves

Parmesan, for grating

1 tbsp good-quality olive oil

80g (3oz) fior di latte mozzarella, torn or sliced

2 slices of good-quality Italian roasted ham

2 tbsp canned sweetcorn (corn)

cracked black pepper

METHOD

1. Preheat the grill (broiler) to its absolute highest setting, and place a large, ovenproof frying pan (skillet) over a high heat and let it get screaming hot.

2. Meanwhile, flatten and stretch the dough ball (following the instructions on page 37) to make a 10-inch pizza base.

3. Lay the pizza base flat in the hot, dry frying pan, then spread with the double cream. Add the basil, a grating of Parmesan and the olive oil, then top with the mozzarella, ham and sweetcorn.

4. Once the base of the pizza has browned, about 1–2 minutes, place the frying pan under the grill on the highest shelf.

5. Once the crust has taken on some colour, about 1–2 minutes, finish with some cracked black pepper.

Mortadella & Pistachio

Mortadella originates in Bologna (AKA 'The Fat City') and is the ham of choice for sandwiches, or panini, across the whole of Italy. It is made by finely mincing pork and incorporating 15% small cubes of pork back fat; our favourite style includes whole toasted pistachios from Bronte in Sicily. We use a pistachio butter (like peanut butter but with pistachios... we know, KNOCK OUT!) to spread across the base of the pizza and cook with mozzarella, Parmesan and basil. We top the cooked pizza with mortadella and spoons of stracciatella (the creamy centre of a burrata). The nuttiness of the pistachio butter, with the saltiness of the mortadella and the cool creaminess of the cheese, is one of our favourite ever combos.

INGREDIENTS

1 ball of Neapolitan pizza dough (see page 36)

40g (1½oz) pistachio butter, let down with 20ml (4 tsp) water

4–5 basil leaves

Parmesan, for grating

1 tbsp good-quality olive oil

60g (2oz) fior di latte mozzarella, torn or sliced

3 slices of mortadella

60g (2oz) burrata or buffalo mozzarella, torn into pieces

30g (1oz) pistachios, lightly toasted and roughly chopped

METHOD

1. Preheat the grill (broiler) to its absolute highest setting, and place a large, ovenproof frying pan (skillet) over a high heat and let it get screaming hot.

2. Meanwhile, flatten and stretch the dough ball (following the instructions on page 37) to make a 10-inch pizza base.

3. Lay the pizza base flat in the hot, dry frying pan, then spread with the pistachio butter. Add the basil, a grating of Parmesan and the olive oil.

4. Once the base of the pizza has browned, about 1–2 minutes, add the mozzarella, then place the frying pan under the grill on the highest shelf.

5. Once the crust has taken on some colour, about 1–2 minutes, top the pizza with the mortadella, burrata and toasted pistachios.

Pumpkin, Sausage, Sage & Chilli

This pizza was inspired by the first man to teach us how to make pizza – Gianluca. He was our cooking teacher when we were in Tuscany and he made a pumpkin and sausage pasta dish that we will remember for ever. We took this recipe as gospel and just transported it onto a pizza, which in our opinion sums up the taste of autumn perfectly.

INGREDIENTS

1 ball of Neapolitan pizza dough
(see page 36)

Parmesan, for grating

1 tbsp good-quality olive oil

80g (3oz) fior di latte mozzarella, torn or sliced

60g (2oz) roasted fennel sausage, cut into bite-sized pieces

4–5 sage leaves

sliced fresh chilli, to taste

chilli oil, to serve

FOR THE PUMPKIN MIXTURE

Makes enough for 4 pizzas

40g (1½oz) butter

50ml (scant ¼ cup) good-quality olive oil

2 garlic cloves, finely diced

500g (1lb 2oz) diced pumpkin
(prepared weight)

salt and freshly ground black pepper

METHOD

1. For the pumpkin, heat the butter, oil and garlic in a large saucepan until the garlic is golden brown. Tip in the pumpkin and cook, stirring occasionally, on a medium heat until soft. Add salt and pepper to taste, then take off the heat and leave to cool.

2. Preheat the grill (broiler) to its absolute highest setting, and place a large, ovenproof frying pan (skillet) over a high heat and let it get screaming hot.

3. Meanwhile, flatten and stretch the dough ball (following the instructions on page 37) to make a 10-inch pizza base.

4. Lay the pizza base flat in the hot, dry frying pan, then spread with 80g (3oz) of the pumpkin mixture. Grate over some Parmesan and drizzle with the olive oil, then top with the mozzarella, sausage, sage leaves and fresh chilli.

5. Once the base of the pizza has browned, about 1–2 minutes, place the frying pan under the grill on the highest shelf.

6. Once the crust has taken on some colour, about 1–2 minutes, drizzle with chilli oil.

Porchetta & Poponcini Peppers

Porchetta, surely the Rolls Royce of Italian hams (or maybe it's more the Humvee?), is originally from a small town called Ariccia, 16 miles south-east of Rome. A suckling pig is completely deboned and sprinkled with a number of things, including salt, lemon zest, rosemary, garlic, fennel seeds, chilli and black pepper. It is then rolled and trussed with string before being slow-cooked over a spit. After about eight hours the skin becomes the most incredible crackling and the meat melt-in-the-mouth tender. Poponcini peppers have an incredible sweet-and-sour flavour, while giving a little heat. This pizza is testament to the benefits of simplicity. Two flavours together on a pizza, perfectly balanced.

INGREDIENTS

1 ball of Neapolitan pizza dough
(see page 36)

80g (3oz) tomato sauce (see page 42)

4–5 basil leaves

Parmesan, for grating

1 tbsp good-quality olive oil

80g (3oz) fior di latte mozzarella, torn or sliced

80g (3oz) thinly sliced porchetta,
torn into pieces

60g (2oz) sweet Gorgonzola, in small pieces

40g (1½oz) drained poponcini peppers

METHOD

1. Preheat the grill (broiler) to its absolute highest setting, and place a large, ovenproof frying pan (skillet) over a high heat and let it get screaming hot.

2. Meanwhile, flatten and stretch the dough ball (following the instructions on page 37) to make a 10-inch pizza base.

3. Lay the pizza base flat in the hot, dry frying pan, then, using a small ladle (or a large spoon), spoon the tomato sauce onto the middle of the pizza. Using the back of the ladle, make concentric circles to spread the sauce, beginning in the middle and finishing 1½in from the edge. Then add the basil, a grating of Parmesan, the olive oil and mozzarella. Top with the porchetta, Gorgonzola and poponcini peppers.

4. Once the base of the pizza has browned, about 1–2 minutes, place the frying pan under the grill on the highest shelf.

5. Once the crust has taken on some colour, about 1–2 minutes, your pizza is ready!

Calzone Ripieno

The calzone can be traced back as far as the Margherita and perhaps even further, when bread dough was stuffed, folded and then deep-fried – AKA pizza fritta, which is the calzone's deep-fried brother (and arguably even more delicious). For our calzone we stick to the Naples traditions. The flavour is completely different to normal pizza because the dough protects the ingredients from the fire of the oven and instead steams them, giving a more delicate flavour.

İNGREDİENTS

1 x 260g (9oz) ball of Neapolitan pizza dough (see page 36)

40g (1½oz) ricotta

80g (3oz) fior di latte mozzarella, torn or sliced

60g (2oz) tomato sauce (see page 42)

Parmesan, for grating

30g (1oz) mushroom mixture (see 62)

60g (2oz) Napoli salami

4–5 basil leaves

1 tbsp good-quality olive oil

METHOD

1. Preheat your oven to its highest temperature. Meanwhile, flatten and stretch the dough ball (following the instructions on page 37) to make a 12-inch pizza base, *without* a pronounced crust.

2. Spread the ricotta over one half of the base. Top with half the mozzarella, then half the tomato sauce, a grating of Parmesan, all of the mushrooms and salami, half the basil and half the olive oil.

3. Fold the un-topped half of the pizza over the topped half and, using your fist, hammer down on the edges to create a tight seal. Use your finger to gently tear a small hole in the top of the calzone to let steam out.

4. Top the pizza with the remaining ingredients and a grating of Parmesan, to create a Margherita pizza on top.

5. Bake in the hot oven until the calzone is golden and charred.

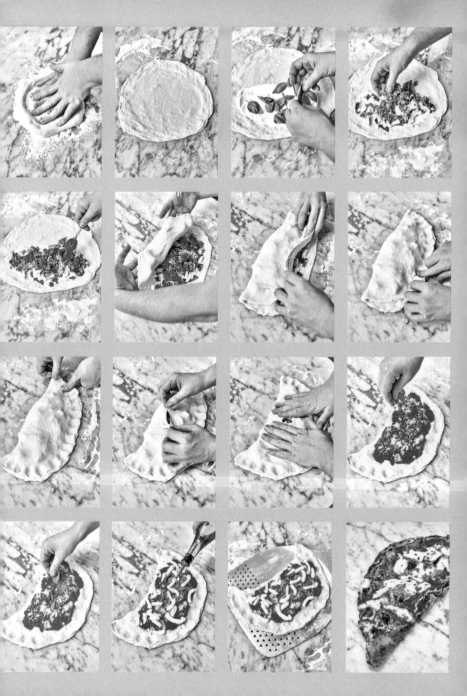

Kale, Anchovy & Chilli

Pizza in January: a battle for the newly health-conscious trying to stick to their New Year's resolutions. So we decided to create a pizza choice on our menu called 'Heaven or Hell'. Two pizzas you could choose from that would send you to heaven or hell. The Americano featured on page 68 played the part of hell and this pizza was the virtuous heaven. Kale's superfood status aside, this is a great combo of earthy anchovy and kale flavours with buffalo mozzarella and a kick of heat from the chilli. We promise it won't disappoint, and it's good for you (ish…), so happy days!

INGREDIENTS

1 ball of Neapolitan pizza dough (see page 36)

80g (3oz) buffalo mozzarella, torn into pieces

Parmesan, for grating

sliced fresh chilli, to taste

1 tbsp good-quality olive oil

chilli oil, to serve

FOR THE KALE AND ANCHOVY

Makes enough for 1 pizza

30g (1oz) kale leaves, roughly sliced

1 tbsp good-quality olive oil

1 garlic clove, chopped

3 anchovy fillets in oil

METHOD

1. Blanch the kale leaves in boiling, salted water for 2–3 minutes until tender, then drain and plunge the leaves into ice-cold water (to retain the colour).

2. Heat the olive oil and garlic in a frying pan until the garlic begins to turn golden. Add the anchovy fillets and cook until they melt into the oil. Add in the drained kale and cook on a medium heat until the kale has taken on all the oil. Take off the heat and leave to cool.

3. Preheat the grill (broiler) to its absolute highest setting, and place a large, ovenproof frying pan (skillet) over a high heat and let it get screaming hot.

4. Meanwhile, flatten and stretch the dough ball (following the instructions on page 37) to make a 10-inch pizza base.

5. Lay the pizza base flat in the hot, dry frying pan then top with 100g (3½oz) of the kale mix, the mozzarella, Parmesan, fresh chilli and olive oil.

6. Once the base of the pizza has browned, about 1–2 minutes, place the frying pan under the grill on the highest shelf.

7. Once the crust has taken on some colour, about 1–2 minutes, drizzle with chilli oil.

Pizza Fiocco

This pizza was invented by Roberto Sustra and his brother, who together run a little pizzeria outside of Naples, in Vomero. He starts with slices of ham on a pizza base, a drizzle of double cream and then uses a potato ricer to 'snow' fine stands of what is essentially mashed potato all over the pizza. He then finishes with grated Parmesan, olive oil and black pepper. As it cooks it creates a beautiful crispy top like a rosti, with a thin layer of light and fluffy potato underneath. If pizza was a hug, this would be it.

INGREDIENTS

1 large potato, peeled

1 ball of Neapolitan pizza dough
(see page 36)

35ml (2½ tbsp) double (heavy) cream

3 slices of prosciutto crudo

80g (3oz) fior di latte mozzarella, torn or sliced

Parmesan, for grating

1 tbsp good-quality olive oil

freshly ground black pepper

METHOD

1. Start by boiling the potato until tender, then drain.

2. Preheat the grill (broiler) to its absolute highest setting, and place a large, ovenproof frying pan (skillet) over a high heat and let it get screaming hot.

3. Meanwhile, flatten and stretch the dough ball (following the instructions on page 37) to make a 10-inch pizza base.

4. Lay the pizza base flat in the hot, dry frying pan, then pour over the cream.

5. Drape the prosciutto slices flat on the base and top with the mozzarella.

6. Using a potato ricer, rice the potato onto the pizza to create one even 'duvet' of a layer that covers the prosciutto.

7. Finish with a generous grating of Parmesan, a drizzle of olive oil and some cracked black pepper.

8. Once the base of the pizza has browned, about 1–2 minutes, place the frying pan under the grill on the highest shelf.

9. Once the crust has taken on some colour, about 1–2 minutes, your hug-in-a-pizza is ready!

Burrata Diavola

We're going to completely come clean here. This was a pizza invented out of necessity, like all good things, right? We'd teamed up with Samsung to create a secret menu for their customers. But, we have to admit, that we completely forgot and 30 minutes before they were about to turn up and taste the creation we had spent so long(!) developing, James was in the kitchen trying to knock something together with the ingredients we had! Starting with a Margherita, he went down a meat lover's angle using our pepperoni and 'nduja, then topped the whole thing off with a mini burrata, our spicy honey and fresh chilli slices. It was a quick fix, but has gone on to be one of our best-selling pizzas. Sorry Team Samsung, if you're reading this... but it all worked out in the end – Bob Dylan wrote *Blowin' in the Wind* in 10 minutes, right?! (Disclaimer: We would like to make it clear that in no way are we comparing a swanky pepperoni pizza to a seminal protest anthem – we just got a little carried away....)

İNGREDİENTS

1 ball of Neapolitan pizza dough (see page 36)

80g (3oz) tomato sauce (see page 42)

4–5 basil leaves

Parmesan, for grating

1 tbsp good-quality olive oil

60g (2oz) 'nduja, ripped into 5–6 blobs

50g (1¾oz) sliced pepperoni

sliced fresh chilli, to taste

80g (3oz) fior di latte mozzarella, torn or sliced

a mini 50g (1¾oz) burrata

spicy honey (see page 48), for drizzling

METHOD

1. Preheat the grill (broiler) to its absolute highest setting, and place a large, ovenproof frying pan (skillet) over a high heat and let it get screaming hot.

2. Meanwhile, flatten and stretch the dough ball (following the instructions on page 37) to make a 10-inch pizza base.

3. Lay the pizza base flat in the hot, dry frying pan, then, using a small ladle (or a large spoon), spoon the tomato sauce onto the middle of the pizza. Using the back of the ladle, make concentric circles to spread the sauce, beginning in the middle and finishing 1½in from the edge. Then add the basil, a grating of Parmesan and the olive oil. Top evenly with the 'nduja pieces, pepperoni slices and fresh chilli.

4. Once the base of the pizza has browned, about 1–2 minutes, add the mozzarella, then place the frying pan under the grill on the highest shelf.

5. Once the crust has taken on some colour, about 1–2 minutes, place a mini burrata in the centre and drizzle with spicy honey.

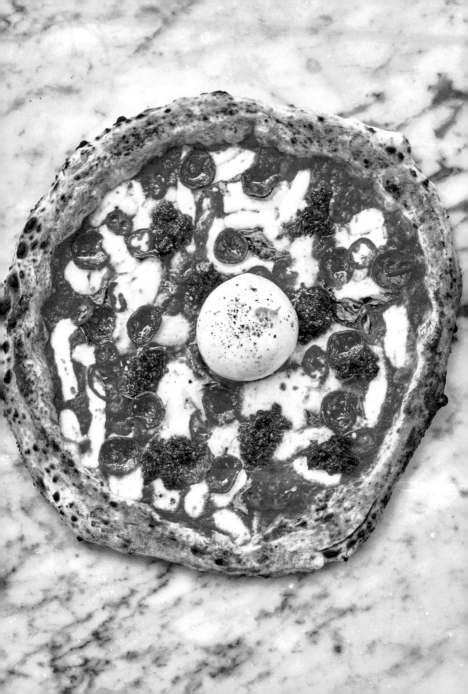

Prosciutto Crudo, Rocket & Parmesan

OK, so we've had time to think about it. Porchetta is definitely the Humvee of hams, leaving the Rolls Royce spot free for infinitely elegant Prosciutto di Parma DOC. We challenge you to add a few thin slices of this amazing cured meat to any pizza and not make it more delicious! We were lucky enough to visit the Prosciutto di Parma factory on our Pizza Pilgrimage and see the painstaking detail that goes into creating this world-renowned ingredient. This pizza is an ode to the Italian classic flavour combo of these three ingredients.

INGREDIENTS

1 ball of Neapolitan pizza dough (see page 36)

80g (3oz) tomato sauce (see page 42)

4–5 basil leaves

Parmesan, for grating, plus 15g (½oz) shavings, to serve

1 tbsp good-quality olive oil, plus extra to finish

80g (3oz) fior di latte mozzarella, torn or sliced

a small handful of rocket (arugula) leaves

3–4 slices of prosciutto crudo

METHOD

1. Preheat the grill (broiler) to its absolute highest setting, and place a large, ovenproof frying pan (skillet) over a high heat and let it get screaming hot.

2. Meanwhile, flatten and stretch the dough ball (following the instructions on page 37) to make a 10-inch pizza base.

3. Lay the pizza base flat in the hot, dry frying pan, then, using a small ladle (or a large spoon), spoon the tomato sauce onto the middle of the pizza. Using the back of the ladle, make concentric circles to spread the sauce, beginning in the middle and finishing 1½in from the edge. Then add the basil, a grating of Parmesan and the tablespoon of olive oil.

4. Once the base of the pizza has browned, about 1–2 minutes, add the mozzarella then place the frying pan under the grill on the highest shelf.

5. Once the crust has taken on some colour, about 1–2 minutes, you have to act fast. Scatter over a bed of rocket, lay the prosciutto slices over the top, then finish by sprinkling the Parmesan shavings over everything and adding a good drizzle of olive oil.

Asparagus & Pancetta

In the UK we grow the most amazing fresh asparagus between the beginning of April and the end of June, and we wanted to celebrate these glorious British spears as best we could. Asparagus' best friend is a good smoky bacon, so we thought it was a great opportunity to marry up one of the UK's best ingredients with one of Italy's – smoked pancetta.

INGREDIENTS

5 asparagus spears

40g (1½oz) cubed smoked pancetta

1 ball of Neapolitan pizza dough (see page 36)

Parmesan, for grating, plus 15g (½oz) shavings, to serve

4–5 basil leaves

80g (3oz) fior di latte mozzarella, torn or sliced

FOR THE LEMON AND PARSLEY OIL

Makes enough for 5 pizzas

50ml (scant ¼ cup) good-quality olive oil

a small handful of chopped parsley

grated zest and juice of ½ lemon

METHOD

1. Start by prepping the asparagus. Snap the tough ends off the spears and discard. Using a swivel peeler, peel the bottom of the asparagus to get rid of any tough skin.

2. Take a high-sided saucepan and, using your asparagus spear as a guide, fill the pan up until only the head of the asparagus is out of the water. Bring to the boil, wrap all the asparagus spears together with an elastic band and place in the water so that only the heads stick out. This will boil the stems and steam the tops, meaning perfect asparagus every time. Once tender, drain and plunge into ice-cold water, to prevent over-cooking.

3. Heat the pancetta in a frying pan and slowly cook down until the fat has rendered out and the pancetta is golden brown.

4. For the lemon and parsley oil, stir together the olive oil, parsley and lemon zest and juice. Leave to infuse.

5. Preheat the grill (broiler) to its absolute highest setting, and place a large, ovenproof frying pan (skillet) over a high heat and let it get screaming hot.

6. Meanwhile, flatten and stretch the dough ball (following the instructions on page 37) to make a 10-inch pizza base.

7. Lay the pizza base flat in the hot, dry frying pan, then add a grating of Parmesan and the basil. Place the asparagus spears over the top and then scatter over the pancetta.

8. Once the base of the pizza has browned, about 1–2 minutes, add the mozzarella then place the frying pan under the grill on the highest shelf.

9. Once the crust has taken on some colour, about 1–2 minutes, drizzle with a tablespoon of the lemon and parsley oil and scatter with Parmesan shavings.

Making NY Slice Pizza at Home

Growing up, New York slice pizza was the food from movies that we most craved. The pepperoni pies delivered by April to the turtles in the sewers, the pizza delivered by Peter Parker, the pizza Rachel orders when she finds out Ross slept with the copy girl. There's something about the NY slice that is so unfussy, that it is the perfect pizza to eat on the sofa while binge-watching *Stranger Things*. (Best. Show. Ever.) Here's our method for recreating this cult classic.

THE DOUGH

650g (4⅔ cups) strong white bread flour, plus extra for dusting

1½ tbsp sugar

3 tsp sea salt

2 tsp instant yeast

450ml (scant 2 cups) lukewarm water

3 tbsp extra-virgin olive oil

THE SAUCE

good-quality olive oil

2 garlic cloves, chopped

2 x 400g (14oz) cans good-quality plum tomatoes

a good pinch each of salt, pepper and sugar

a good pinch of dried oregano

a handful of chopped basil

THE TOPPİNG

semi-dry grated mozzarella (placed in the freezer for 20 minutes)

METHOD

1. Mix the flour, sugar, salt and yeast in a food processor. Quickly pulse until the ingredients are incorporated. Add the water and olive oil, then pulse until the dough forms a ball that rides around the bowl above the blade, about 30 seconds.

2. Knead the dough on a lightly floured surface until smooth. Divide the dough into two even balls and pop into two individual freezer bags. Place in the fridge and allow to prove for at least 24–48 hours.

3. Heat a glug of olive oil in a saucepan. Add the garlic and gently fry until golden brown. Add the tomatoes, salt, pepper, sugar, oregano and basil. Gently cook the tomato sauce with a lid on for 1 hour until the tomatoes have broken down and you have a deep-flavoured sauce. Leave to cool.

4. Two hours before you're ready for pizza, take the dough out the fridge and shape into balls by gathering the dough towards the bottom and pinching it. Flour well and place each ball in a separate bowl. Cover tightly with clingfilm (plastic wrap) and allow to rise in a warm spot until doubled in size.

5. One hour before pizza time, preheat your oven as hot as it will go. Place a pizza stone or baking sheet in the oven.

6. Stretch one of your dough balls into a circle, into a 14-inch base, leaving a 1-inch crust. Transfer to a chopping board.

7. Spoon half the sauce onto your base and evenly spread, avoiding the crust. Top with some semi-frozen mozzarella.

8. Slide your pizza into the oven and cook for 10–12 minutes until the crust is browned and the cheese has melted. Slice.

9. Repeat with the other dough ball and remaining sauce and mozzarella.

'THERE'S NO BETTER FEELING İN THE WORLD THAN A WARM PİZZA BOX ON YOUR LAP.' PAUL BLART, MALL COP

Pizza dudes at Forcella Pizza,
Lorimer, NYC.

Crust Dippers

A totally American invention that we have adopted in our pizzerias to help promote the love of the crust and to avoid the pizza cardinal sin of not eating your crusts. Here are five ideas for crust dippers you can make quickly and easily at home. But first things first, let's get a basic mayonnaise recipe down…

BASIC MAYO (AKA YOUR CRUST DIPPER FLAVOUR VEHICLE)

Add one or two egg yolks to a mixing bowl. Give it a quick whisk to break them up, then take a combo of neutral flavoured oil (we like sunflower) and enough extra-virgin olive oil to impart some flavour but without overpowering with bitter flavour. Begin to slowly trickle the oils into the bowl, whisking vigorously using a balloon whisk (add the oil very gradually to begin with as this is when the mayo is most likely to split). Once it starts to thicken, you can increase the flow of oil. You want to add enough oil so that when you pick up the whisk the mayo does not run off. This is to add maximum 'mayo grab' to the crust. Once you have your basic emulsion, add a little salt and pepper to taste; we also add a splash of lemon juice to give a little acidity. From here you have a blank canvas to make whatever crust dippers you want. Go for your life. Nothing is off limits.

WHITE TRUFFLE

For this you're going to have to hunt down your local Italian deli or maybe head online. In Italy they make an incredible '*crema di funghi con tartufo*', which is a slow-cooked mushroom paste with truffle. In the pizzerias we use this paste as a base by adding it to our mayo mix; the paste adds an amazing umami flavour as well as colour, with beautiful flecks of mushroom and truffle. To ramp up the truffle flavour, we then add extra white truffle oil to taste.

PESTO

If it's possible, this is even simpler. We use a fresh basil leaf pesto from our friends at Belazu to mix with our mayo base to make a thick, creamy pesto dipper that is hands down our best seller.

'NDUJA

This is one for the spicy meat lovers! We get hands-on by skinning an 'nduja, donning a pair of *Breaking Bad*-style gloves and massaging the 'nduja until we have a soft paste that has been slightly warmed by our hands and is therefore releasing some oils. We then add the mayo base and again massage the 'nduja into the mayo with our hands. The result is a bright red, deep, meaty and intensely flavoured 'nduja dipper.

SALSA VERDE

For this we don't use a mayo base but make a classic salsa verde. Take big bunches of all your favourite fresh herbs. We use basil, parsley, a little mint, fresh oregano and rosemary. To use the technical term: 'Chop the hell out of them' until you have really fine flecks of herbs. In a bowl, mix some good-quality olive oil, a couple of anchovy fillets that have been pulverised using the side of the knife, some chopped capers, grated lemon zest, salt and pepper and a little lemon juice. Add the herbs and combine until you have a thick mixture that is shiny and just drops off a spoon. Taste for seasoning and add more salt and lemon juice if it needs it. (FYI this is an awesome sauce to serve with chicken, fish, veggies… basically anything!)

ARRABBİATA

Heat some good-quality olive oil in a pan and chuck in a couple of whole, fat garlic cloves that have been smashed under the back of a knife. Sauté for a couple of minutes, then add as many chilli flakes as you dare. Cook for another minute, fish out the garlic cloves, then add a couple of cans of plum tomatoes. Lower the heat and cook until the tomatoes have reduced by at least a third and broken down to a smooth sauce. Check the seasoning and add salt and sugar to taste. Don't forget that when the sauce cools, the flavours will dull down slightly, so be bold! You can serve this hot too, but we think cold works best as a crust dipper.

PESTO

SALSA VERDE

'NDUJA

WHITE TRUFFLE

ARRABBIATA

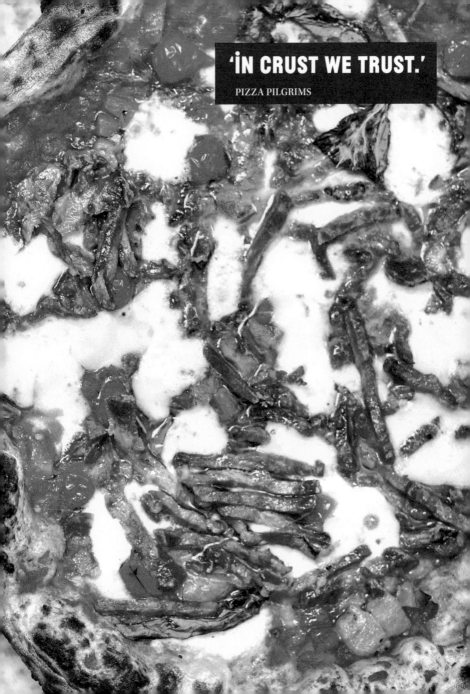

'IN CRUST WE TRUST.'

PIZZA PILGRIMS

Pizza Soup

Just bear with us...

When we opened our third pizzeria on London's Exmouth Market, we had the opportunity to re-establish a market stall outside our shop. We opened in the dead of winter – and we wanted to come up with something to 'warm the cockles' and which was linked to, but not exactly, pizza. Enter, pizza soup. Essentially a deconstructed pizza – the idea was a simple tomato and basil soup, served with individual mini mozzarella and Parmesan calzones. It was truly delicious and fun, as well as really easy to make. We kept the stall throughout the winter – but seemingly the world was not quite ready for pizza soup in 2015. Maybe now is its time!

FOR THE SOUP

Serves 2

3 garlic cloves, peeled
drizzle of good-quality olive oil
3 heaped tsp tomato paste
2 x 400g (14oz) cans chopped tomatoes
large pinch each of salt and sugar
2 large handfuls of basil leaves

FOR THE MİNİ CALZONE

1 ball of Neapolitan pizza dough
(see page 36)
buffalo mozzarella
Parmesan, for grating

METHOD

1. Preheat your oven to its hottest setting.

2. Fry the garlic cloves in the olive oil in a large pan over a medium heat. After 3 minutes, add the tomato paste and cook, stirring, for 2 minutes, before adding the canned tomatoes. Add the salt and sugar, and simmer for 15 minutes. Taste and check for seasoning, then take off the heat and stir in the basil leaves.

3. While the soup is simmering, cut the dough ball in half and create a mini pizza base with each, following the method on page 37.

4. Tear off two or three bite-sized pieces of mozzarella per calzone and place on one half of the pizza bases.

5. Fold the bases in half, sealing around the edge, then grate some Parmesan over the top of each.

6. Bake in the oven for 10 minutes, or until taking on some colour.

7. Serve the soup in bowls with the mini calzone alongside.

Chilli Oil

A few summers ago we headed out to Calabria, the very southern tip of Italy and the spiritual home of Italian chilli. We took some of the team from our pizzerias to the annual Peperoncino Festival in Diamante. The goal of the trip was to get some first-hand experience of the 'high' that you feel when you eat lots of chilli.

The festival was mad. Hundreds of stalls lined the beach serving every single product or dish you could imagine, but laced with chilli. We started off slow but soon worked our way up to the big leagues when we found a guy selling what he called 'Calabrian Nutella'. He handed us a teaspoon of it and, once we'd eaten it, he told us it was pure Carolina Reaper chilli paste, with a cool 2.2 million on the Scoville heat scale. It hits you like a bus, and all of a sudden your mouth is on fire and you begin to panic. For about five minutes we were genuinely scared, but as the pain begins to plateau, and the rising fear of death begins to pass, you start to feel amazing! The rest of the evening was a bit of a blur but there is a video on our YouTube channel of the night, which is worth a watch.

When we got home, we wanted to create a chilli oil that would replicate this feeling, and this is the recipe we settled on. A really good kick but with the fruity flavour of the Carolina Reaper chilli, and garlic and smoked paprika for flavour.

INGREDIENTS

Makes about 500ml/2 cups

500ml (generous 2 cups) good-quality, light olive oil

50g (1¾oz) garlic, very finely chopped

1 fresh Carolina Reaper chilli

50g (1¾oz) dried Calabrian chilli flakes

10g (⅓oz) smoked paprika

METHOD

1. Put the olive oil, garlic and the whole chilli (ensuring to prick with a knife so it doesn't explode on you!) in a saucepan.

2. Cook on a low heat until the garlic has gone a light golden brown and the chilli has softened.

3. Remove the pan from the heat and add the chilli flakes and smoked paprika.

4. Stir well and leave to cool. Decant into a clean bottle along with all of the bits in the pan, if possible. This chilli oil is good for use for up to 3 weeks.

The Nutella Ring

Nutella was invented in 1946 by Pietro Ferrero, who started adding hazelnuts to his chocolate in World War II to compensate for sugar rationing. It took him another 10 years to add lecithin to make his hazelnut chocolate spreadable – and he was off to the races. It is reported by the BBC that Nutella is now enjoyed in 160 countries, and 365 million kilos are devoured per year worldwide. That's a million kilos a day, or the weight of the Empire State Building, across the whole year.

Nutella is almost a way of life in Italy. Pretty much every single kid grows up eating Nutella with *cornetto* (croissant), *grissini* (breadsticks), in white bread sandwiches, on ice cream, and even in espresso.

At the pizzerias we make a Nutella and salted ricotta pizza ring that has been a best seller since the pizza-van days. We stretch out a long rectangle of pizza dough, then lay down a fat line of Nutella and ricotta. We finish with a sprinkle of sea salt just to up the addictiveness, then fold the dough over to create a Nutella stuffed snack. We then bring the ends together to make a ring and bake it in the pizza oven. It's served with a ball of vanilla gelato. Something about the salty dough and the sweet Nutella makes this criminally addictive!

INGREDIENTS

130g (4½oz) Neapolitan pizza dough
(see page 36)

40g (1½oz) ricotta

about 100g (3½oz) Nutella

sea salt

ice cream, to serve

METHOD

1. Preheat your oven as hot as it will go.
2. Using your fingertips, stretch out the dough into a long rectangle about 35cm/14in long and 12cm/5in wide.
3. Using a spoon, spread the ricotta over the dough lengthways in a long line. Then spoon as much Nutella as you can onto the dough in a long line down the middle of the ricotta. Sprinkle with sea salt.
4. Fold the dough over itself lengthways so you have a long Nutella parcel, then, using a closed fist, hammer the long edge to ensure a really strong seal on the dough.
5. Bring the ends of the parcel around to create a ring (with the seam on the inside) and press the two ends of dough together, using your fist again to make a strong seal.
6. Bake until the ring has inflated and the crust is golden. Serve with vanilla ice cream.

NUTELLA FUN FACTS

- Nutella buys 25% of the world's hazelnut supply every year: over 100,000 tons.

- Each 400g (14oz) jar of Nutella contains 52 hazelnuts.

- World Nutella Day is 5th February.

- In 2013, some sweet-toothed bandits pulled off a heist on a Nutella lorry, stealing 5 metric tonnes of the stuff, worth an estimated £20,000.

- Italy loves Nutella so much that in 2014 they commemorated it on a postage stamp. Does that make Nutella the Queen of Italy?!

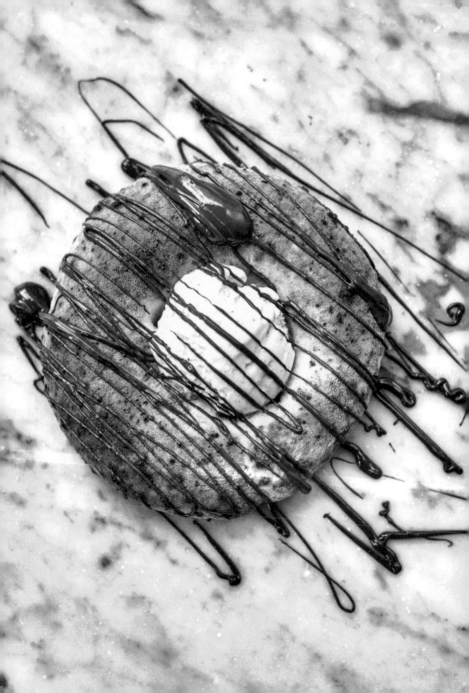

Calzonification

Yeah, it's a real word for sure.

kal.zone.if.ik.ay.she.un
verb. the act of wrapping chocolate bars in pizza dough and baking them in the oven.

In 2017, we opened our pizzeria in London's Shoreditch and were looking for a fun way to bring it to the attention of the local area. The Nutella Ring (see page 106) had long been a big part of our menu and, as such, we decided to explore what other chocolatey treats could be improved by wrapping them in dough. We made a short YouTube video about our exploits which got over 20 million views in just a couple of weeks. Fair to say we were on to something!

We experimented with a selection of chocolate bars and confectionery combinations, and here are a few of our findings:

MARS & REESE'S PIECES

Like a Snickers on speed, this melty, caramelly, nutty dream is guaranteed to make you happy (while shaving a few years off your life).

QUALITY STREET

This takes Forrest Gump's mum's famous quip about a box of chocolates and really ups the ante. Bite-sized morsels of chocolate with an element of surprise every single time. Brilliant fun.

CREME EGG

In a similar vein to the chip shops in the UK that will deep-fry a creme egg for you, the dough adds a salty layer to the famous Easter sugar hit, and elevates it to another level.

KINDER BUENO

The real game changer here is the crunch from the Bueno bar. To really spice this one up, throw in a couple of Kinder Surprise eggs to the mix (after you have taken the prizes out of course).

WARNING: HARIBO STAR MIX

We'd like to confirm that this combo doesn't work AT ALL. Pizza dough and Haribo should forever be kept apart. You heard it here first.

Pizza Equations

It must be true, it's maths.

Pizza and maths have, in the past, rarely found joint airtime. But actually, listening hard in your maths classes at school might have informed your pizza eating for the rest of your life. What is also clear is that some of the top mathematical minds have been using pizza for many years to give their high-level research some healthy PR value!

The first thing to observe, which is almost proof that a higher power exists, is the formula for working out the exact size of the pizza in front of you. If you take a circular pizza with generic depth 'a' and generic radius 'z' (the distance from the centre to the edge) then the actual equation to work out the amount of pizza you have is:

$$Pi\,(\pi) \times z \times z \times a$$

Which is just too glorious, no? But who cares, we hear (some of) you ask. Well, using this formula you can actually prove some interesting stuff. For example, you wouldn't think so, but an 18-inch pizza is actually bigger than two entire 12-inch pizzas. So, think about that next time you go for a large or a medium...

Finally, Joel Haddley and Stephen Worsley from the University of Liverpool have worked out that the most scientifically accurate way to cut pizza fairly into 12 slices is the distinctly un-fun sounding 'monohedral disc tiling' method. Shown opposite, these cuts will produce scientifically perfect, equal slices. There's just one glaring omission: half the slices will be almost entirely crust! Dough!

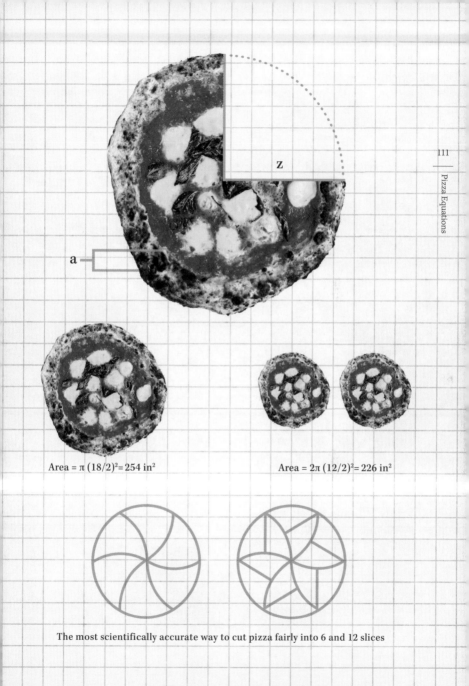

a

z

Area = $\pi (18/2)^2 = 254$ in^2

Area = $2\pi (12/2)^2 = 226$ in^2

The most scientifically accurate way to cut pizza fairly into 6 and 12 slices

Eating Pizza

How do you eat yours?

Walking through our pizzeria we see it all. People from every walk of life eating pizza in every imaginable way. How you eat your slice is the true inkblot test of the pizza world. On the next few pages, we've outlined eight pizza-eating techniques we see people using and asked the UK's leading body language specialist, Adrianne Carter (AKA 'The Face Whisperer'), to give us an insight into what pizza-eating styles reveal about the type of person you are. So, get ready to understand yourself a little better...

THE NEAPOLİTAN HANDS-FREE

Poor old Bill De Blasio, the New York Mayor, was given no end of stick for eating his pizza with a knife and fork. The truth is, the OG pizza eaters in Naples always eat with a knife and fork. The reasoning goes that pizza is too important to rush, and you should sit down, relax with a good glass of wine and take the time to enjoy your pizza (with a knife and fork!).

The Face Whisperer: This person will be conscious of not making a mess and keeping their hands and face as clean as possible. They are probably the tidiest person in the house and office and like to do things properly and in a set way.

THE CİGAR

We see this a lot in our pizzerias, and the people that do it always look in-the-know. The main benefit here is supposed to be that, in every mouthful, you get a bit of everything, from crust to sauce to cheese. You roll the slice from the tip to the crust to create a 'cigar', then eat it from top to bottom. The jury's out on this one for us. Surely you want to celebrate every part of the pizza separately?!

The Face Whisperer: The term 'party pooper' definitely springs to mind. This pizza eater sounds like the person who takes all the fun and enjoyment out of a party. They're also likely to be constantly in a rush, having to absorb a lot of info at once.

THE BLOTTER

We love that scene in *Along Came Polly* when Philip Seymour Hoffman coaches Ben Stiller on pizza grease after Stiller's character blots his slice with napkins to reduce the oil. There are two problems with the blot: 1. Hoffman's character is right, the grease has all the flavour; 2. The napkins you get at a NY slice joint are about as absorbent as clingfilm (plastic wrap). If you have to take some of the oil off, the only technique is to hold the slice up in the air and squeeze it like you're milking a cow (but this makes you look like a weirdo, so we wouldn't advise it!).

The Face Whisperer: This person is scared to enjoy themselves and is likely to worry about all sorts of things. It's time to stop worrying and eat the pizza, oil and all!

THE NEAPOLITAN PIZZA BOAT

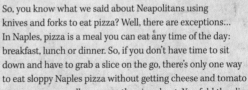

So, you know what we said about Neapolitans using knives and forks to eat pizza? Well, there are exceptions... In Naples, pizza is a meal you can eat any time of the day: breakfast, lunch or dinner. So, if you don't have time to sit down and have to grab a slice on the go, there's only one way to eat sloppy Naples pizza without getting cheese and tomato all over you: the pizza boat. You fold the slice in half, then tuck the end over, creating a vessel for the cheese and sauce that ensures no leakage. True pro stuff.

The Face Whisperer: A person who wants to ensure they don't miss a bit of the good stuff or make a mess. Probably Mr or Mrs Practical in their daily life, and the person we all turn to for a practical solution to our everyday problems.

THE SNAG AND DRAG

In our pizza lives, we have only ever seen this once, and we can still see the guy who did it, clear as day, sitting in our pizzeria. An older man of about 60 came in, ordered a Margherita and, when it arrived, picked up the plate, grabbed the pizza with his teeth, pulled it towards him and began to work his way through it straight off the plate. It was much like watching a snake eat a baby deer, and we respect him for that...

The Face Whisperer: This person does not care what other people think of how they behave or what they do. Possibly has no friends to monitor their behaviour.

THE REVERSE SHUFFLE

Crusts first. We don't know about you, but we just don't trust this method. Based on what we see in our pizzerias, we think about 1 in 20 people prefer to eat on the dark side. Our theory is this: these people are those who like the crust the least, and therefore want to get it over with as soon as possible. The main issue here is that you lose the handle god gave pizza and end up with sauce all over your hands. Hmmm...

The Face Whisperer: This is the rebellious pizza eater. The one who wants to do things differently and not follow the crowd – even when it's impractical to do so.

CRUST LEAVER

There's only one thing worse than eating the crusts first... not eating them at all! We feel this must be a hangover from when you were a kid and your mum would tell you to eat the crusts of your sandwich. Some people are really down on the crust of a pizza but, the truth is, if it's a good pizza the crust is the best bit! Also, by not eating the crusts you're wasting almost half the pizza! Poor form in our book...

The Face Whisperer: This suggests the kind of person who can never be bothered to finish a task, and often ducks out at the last minute. There are probably a lot of DIY projects in their house that get started but never finished!

THE TONY MANERO

Depending on when you were born, this technique can also be referred to as "The Joey Special" (from *Friends*). In 1978 John Travolta put Brooklyn pizza on the big screen when he played the role of Tony Manero in *Saturday Night Fever* – the paint-slinging disco fiend with a penchant for good pizza. His special move? Stacking one slice on top of the other and eating both in one go. Combine this with a flare-fuelled strut and you have one of the most iconic pizza scenes in movie history.

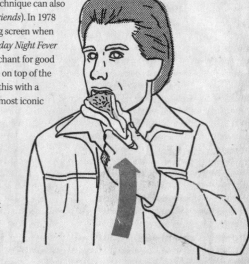

The Face Whisperer: Double enjoyment! One flavour or two? In going for the same flavour on both slices, this person knows what they like in life and aren't afraid to enjoy it! Different topping combos on each slice reveal a person who isn't afraid to mix things up and is always looking to max out their enjoyment. They also possibly suffer from FOMO...

James doing the Tony Manero at Lombardi's, Manhattan.

What to Drink with Pizza

Some tips for loading up that Globe bar at home...

Count Camillo Negroni, what a guy. From posh Italian stock, he consistently bucked tradition. Travelling across America, spending some time as a cowboy, then living in London, learning to love gin. He then headed home to his favourite bar, Caffè Casoni, in Florence, Italy in 1919. It was here he decided his Americano cocktail wasn't packing the punch, so he asked his bartender to strengthen it up by switching the soda for gin. It became an instant hit and is still one of the best ways to kick off a good night. Here's our recipe for the classic and a couple of twists to have a go at.

NEGRONI

The original and the best...

> 25ml (1fl oz) Campari
> 25ml (1fl oz) London dry gin
> 25ml (1fl oz) Martini Rosso
> slice of orange, to garnish

Fill a whisky tumbler with ice. Pour over your alcohols and stir.

Add the orange garnish and drink. Make another...

'A NEGRONI IS A PERFECT DRINK AS FAR AS I'M CONCERNED... THAT FIRST SIP IS CONFUSING AND NOT PARTICULARLY PLEASANT. BUT MAN, IT GROWS ON YOU.'

ANTHONY BOURDAIN

NEGRONI BIANCO

This is the meekest and mildest of the negroni family. Perfect as a 'sundowner' cocktail while riding a giant inflatable swan across an infinity pool... we reckon.

    25ml (1fl oz) Cocchi Bianco vermouth
    25ml (1fl oz) London dry gin
    25ml (1fl oz) Luxardo Bitter Bianco liqueur
    twist of grapefruit peel, to garnish

Fill a whisky tumbler with ice. Pour over your alcohols and stir.

Add the grapefruit garnish and drink.

PEPPERGRONI

How do you go about making a negroni better? Well, we answered that age-old question by adding Bourbon and garnishing with pepperoni slices. Job done.

This is a slightly sweeter and smokier variation on the classic, so it's good for people who don't like the really bitter notes of negronis. And, of course, people who are just looking to get more pepperoni in their lives...

    25ml (1fl oz) Campari
    25ml (1fl oz) Knob Creek (or your
    favourite) Bourbon
    25ml (1fl oz) Martini Rosso
    3 slices of pepperoni on a cocktail stick,
    to garnish

Fill a whisky tumbler with ice. Pour over your alcohols and stir.

Add the pepperoni garnish and drink.

Limoncello

Limoncello can often fall into the same bracket as a holiday friendship – you make an acquaintance on a sunny beach somewhere and think, this is a lifelong friendship. Then you realise, when you are drinking it warm on a Tuesday night with take-out, that it's not as great as you thought it was.

That said, when not purchased in a bottle in the shape of a stiletto heel – or the shape of Italy – limoncello can be delicious. Really, truly, finish-off-the-bottle delicious. If you have ever been to Naples or the Amalfi coast, you know this to be true. And given it was invented around the bay of Naples, you can bet it goes well with a pizza!

Despite being the second favourite liqueur in Italy (after Campari) it has not really travelled the world to a great extent. It was this exact issue – the difficulty of getting hold of a good limoncello for the pizzerias – that led us to make our own, from amazing Amalfi lemons (sourced from the Aceto groves above the town of Amalfi) and award-winning Chase vodka from Herefordshire.

So, we guess our message here is, shop with caution. You are looking for a limoncello in a non-novelty bottle, with a pale yellow colour (not luminous) and an opaque liquid (highlighting a high level of lemon essential oil). It is also worth looking for one made with real Amalfi lemons – only these contain the full density of oil in the skins to make a great product. Just saying: our Pococello (pococello.com) ticks all the boxes!

What is also surprising is how versatile limoncello is...

LIMONCELLO SPRITZ

A great alternative to an Aperol Spritz, this is a super-refreshing (and super-Italian) way to while away those summer nights.

> 50ml (3 tbsp) good-quality limoncello
>
> 125ml (½ cup) prosecco
>
> 20ml (4 tsp) sparkling water
>
> sprig of rosemary, to garnish

Pour over ice and serve with the rosemary.

LIMONCELLO & TONIC

This is a lower-ABV, sweeter version of a gin and tonic.

> 50ml (3 tbsp) good-quality limoncello
>
> 125ml (½ cup) tonic water
>
> slice of lemon, to garnish

Serve over ice.

Luigi Aceto, the lemon man of Amalfi.

İCE-COLD LİMONCELLO SHOTS

One for the purist: this is the original way to drink shots (and happily the fastest). Keep your limoncello (and your shot glasses) in the freezer and enjoy quickly!

Spritzes

APEROL SPRITZ

This has exploded out of Italy recently. It is huge in Venice, but its lurid orangey goodness is now just as comfortable on the streets of Shoreditch or Williamsburg. Try it straight with white wine rather than prosecco, or for a more grown-up version replace the Aperol with Campari. The classic way to serve this is as a 3, 2, 1:

3 parts prosecco (or white wine)

2 parts Aperol (or Campari)

1 part sparkling water

slice of orange, to garnish

Serve over ice.

ELDERFLOWER SPRITZ

Another classic Italian flavour profile recreated as a spritz – the classy choice!

50ml (3 tbsp) elderflower liqueur

125ml (½ cup) prosecco

25ml (scant 2 tbsp) sparkling water

slice of lemon, to garnish

Serve over ice.

CYNAR SPRITZ

We are keen to meet the person who decided to create a liqueur out of artichoke hearts – that must have been a very late-night plan. However, Cynar is actually delicious – albeit ferociously bitter. If you need to wimp out, dilute with prosecco!

50ml (3 tbsp) Cynar liqueur

125ml (½ cup) prosecco

25ml (scant 2 tbsp) sparkling water

Serve over ice.

Italian Beer

Italy has (like almost every nation on earth) really gone all-out on craft beers in the last few years. This from a country which, for all its amazing elegance, haute couture and style, still sees Tennent's Super as the height of sophistication (it will often be at the top of a beer list in a posh restaurant or swanky bar).

Anyway – there are many, many other better options available, and it seemed appropriate for pizza beer to be Italian. So here are a couple of our favourites...

BIRRA DEL BORGO

We visited this fantastic craft brewery, just outside of Rome, in 2015 on our second pilgrimage through Italy. They are lovely people – and genuinely come up with some fantastic (and completely off-the-wall) beers. We love the hoppy Reale, their Lisa lager is delicious and refreshing, and their constant wheel of creativity means there is always something new to try (oyster beer anyone?). The bottle is iconic also – we have served it in our pizzerias for almost five years now and it is universally loved.

BIRRA MORETTI

Not exactly a 'craft beer' – this lager brand has been owned by Heineken for many years and is growing fast. However, it is a great beer for food, and in our mind is a nicer fit for pizza than the other lager monster from Italy – Peroni.

Wine

Iced Tea

NEAPOLiTAN WiNE

Although not famed for its wine, Campania has some ancient wineries that produce great wines. One of those is Lacryma Christi – or 'The Tears of Christ' (classic understated name) – a white based around the Falanghina grape grown in the foothills of Mount Vesuvius. It's often mentioned historically, including in Alexandre Dumas' *The Count of Monte Cristo*.

If reds are your thing, the grape to look for is Aglianico – a favourite of the Romans and the Greeks. It is used to make Taurasi – one of Campania's leading red wines.

LAMBRUSCO

Bear with us on this one. Lambrusco is a sweet, red, sparkling wine – served chilled much like prosecco. Although that sounds bonkers, it is delicious and fantastic with pizza. The tannic quality cuts through the cheese and dough a treat. Make sure you warn people before you serve it, or they might think you've lost it.

WiNE & PiZZA PAiRiNG

Margherita: Go for a red wine with acidity and lots of fruit – maybe Barbera d'Asti, Frappato or Beaujolais Cru. Lighter reds like Gamay are also a good bet. If you go for wines that are too heavy the tannins can clash with the tomato, leaving a metallic taste in the mouth.

Pepperoni/meat: Spicy meats can probably take a wine with a little more punch: Syrah or Nero D'Avola from Sicily will work well.

White Pizza: With no tomato sauce, turn to white wine. Good options here are Soave, Pinot Grigio or Verdicchio.

OUR HOUSE SHAKEN iCED TEAS

Every kid growing up in Italy loves Estathé, the little plastic cups of iced tea with the film lid and the straw you have to stab through the top. We wanted a couple of iced teas on our menu, to give our Italian customers that nostalgic hit. Our two favourites are Earl Grey & elderflower, and builders' tea & peach. The options are limitless though, so go nuts!

    1 tea bag of your choice

    125ml (½ cup) boiling water

    375ml (1½ cups) cold water

    50ml (3 tbsp) cordial of choice

    30ml (2 tbsp) lemon juice

    slice of lemon, to garnish

Steep the teabag in the boiling water for two minutes. Remove the tea bag and top up with the cold water. Add the cordial and lemon juice. Fill a cocktail shaker with ice and pour in the tea mix. Shake the hell out of it and serve over ice with a slice of lemon.

'I LOVE PIZZA, MEANING: EVEN WHEN I'M IN THE MIDDLE OF EATING PIZZA, I WISH I WERE EATING PIZZA.'

JANDY NELSON

Index

Managing Director
Sarah Lavelle

Commissioning Editor
Harriet Webster

Head of Design
Claire Rochford

Art Direction and Design
Dave Brown

Design Assistant
Gemma Hayden

Photographer
Dave Brown

Head of Production
Stephen Lang

Production Controller
Martina Georgieva

This edition first published in 2023 by Quadrille,
an imprint of Hardie Grant Publishing

Text is extracted and updated from *Pizza* by James and Thom Elliot

Quadrille
52–54 Southwark Street
London SE1 1UN
quadrille.com

Text © Pizza Pilgrims 2023
Photography © Dave Brown 2020
Design and layout © Quadrille 2023

Select cover illustrations © Dave Brown 2023 / p.1 © Ivana Zorn 2020 / pp.20,23
© Andy Rash 2020 / p.26 © Pizza Pilgrims Ltd 2020 / p.27 © Lateef Photography
2020 / p.31 © Pizza Pilgrims Ltd 2020 / p.37 © Pizza Pilgrims Ltd 2020 / p.39 ©
Lateef Photography 2020 / p.111 background: Old homework papers/Paper Farms/
Creative Market / pp.112–115 © Tobatron 2020 / p.118 © Pizza Pilgrims Ltd 2020

ISBN: 978 1 78713 971 8

Printed in China

MIX
Paper from
responsible sources
FSC™ C020056